Bermuda

D0627835

SEA
DIVING

the
Bermuda Triangle

APA PUBLICATIONS

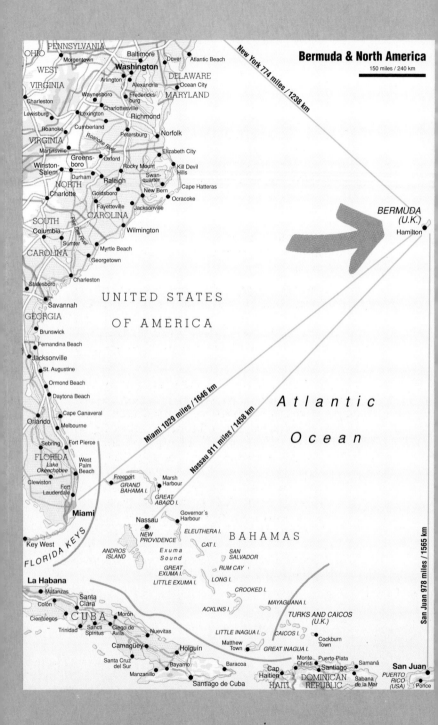

Dear Visitor!

Turquoise waters, pink-tinged beaches and picturesque fishing boats are enough to entice many visitors to Bermuda. Others come to play on some of the best golf courses in the world – and to enjoy unparalleled scenery while they do so. Some simply enjoy relaxing in a tranquil atmosphere, surrounded by unusually friendly people, amid a landscape sprinkled with white-roofed cottages and hedgerows of red hibiscus and pink oleander. Many are intrigued by a place so free of pollution that the rainfall remains sparkling, crystal clear and entirely drinkable.

In the following pages our Insight correspondent will help you make the best use of a short stay on this tiny island, by ensuring that you get to see and enjoy all the sights and activities you have heard about and discover lots more that you had not even dreamed of.

 David F Raine is a writer and historian who has lived in Bermuda for more than 30 years and has already written three books about various aspects of the island's history. He has been here for so long he can hardly remember what it was that first attracted him: the perennially green undergrowth, the perfect climate, the vivid flora or just the convivial atmosphere. But he is equally enthusiastic about all facets of Bermudian life and hopes to share his enthusiasm with you as he guides you around the island, giving you an insider's view of the place he loves, plus a brief background history, and lots of practical tips to help make your stay trouble-free and wholly enjoyable.

Hans Höfer
Publisher, Insight Guides

C O N T E N T S

Pages 2/3:
Horseshoe
Bay

Pages 10/11:
Needle and Thread
Alley, St George

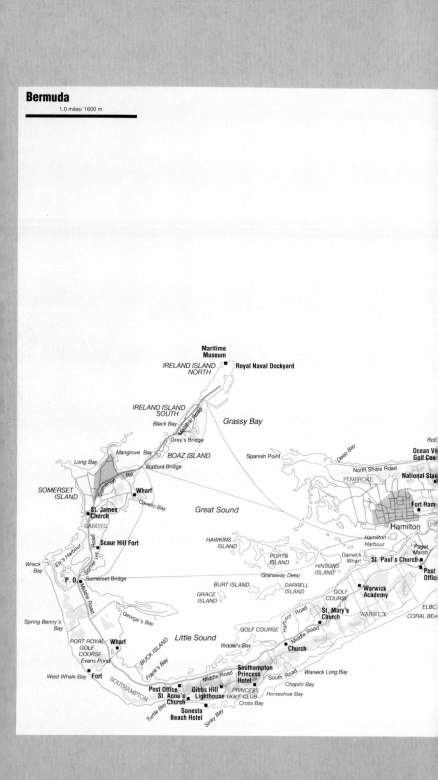

Bermuda

1.0 miles/ 1600 m

Maritime Museum
Royal Naval Dockyard
IRELAND ISLAND NORTH

IRELAND ISLAND SOUTH
Black Bay
Grassy Bay
Melbur Road
Grey's Bridge
Mangrove Bay
BOAZ ISLAND
Spanish Point
Deep Bay
Rob
Ocean Vi
Golf Cou
Watford Bridge
North Shore Road
Long Bay
Somerset Rd.
PEMBROKE
National Sta
Wharf
Cavello Bay
Fort Ham
SOMERSET ISLAND
St. James Church
SANDYS
Great Sound
Hamilton
Scaur Hill Fort
HAWKINS ISLAND
Hamilton Harbour
PORT'S ISLAND
Darrell's Wharf
St. Paul's Church
Paget Marsh
Wreck Bay
Ely's Harbour
Somerset Road
HINSONS ISLAND
Post Offic
P. O.
Somerset Bridge
Granaway Deep
BURT ISLAND
DARRELL ISLAND
GRACE ISLAND
GOLF COURSE
Warwick Academy
Middle Road
George's Bay
Little Sound
Harbour Road
St. Mary's Church
WARWICK
ELBC
CORAL BE
PORT ROYAL GOLF COURSE
Wharf
BUCK ISLAND
GOLF COURSE
Riddel's Bay
Church
Evans Pond
Frank's Bay
Middle Road
West Whale Bay
Fort
Spring Benny's Bay
Southampton Princess Hotel
South Road
Warwick Long Bay
SOUTHAMPTON
Post Office
St. Anne's Church
Gibbs Hill Lighthouse
PRINCESS GOLF CLUB
Chaplin Bay
Horseshoe Bay
Turtle Bay
Sonesta Beach Hotel
Cross Bay
Sinky Bay

The Isle of Devils

The Islands of Bermuda first appeared on a map dated 1511. They were named after the Spanish explorer Juan de Bermudez who had first sighted them eight years earlier but had been frightened off by hostile birds, later identified as cahows. The crew of another ship, captained by Diego Ramirez, which ran aground opposite what is now Spanish Point, were also terrified by these creatures who 'came to us... uttering a multitudinous chorus of cries', and which they associated with the devil. The sailors soon discovered that the birds were easy to catch and good to eat, but Bermuda still gained the title of the Isle of Devils.

When Bermudez returned to these same waters in 1514 he still did not touch land; instead, his chronicler Oviedo y Valdes seemed content to comment on the abundance of fish and bird life, without any desire to put his foot on 'the furthest of all islands that are found at this day in the world'. A handcut rock-carving dated

17th-century map

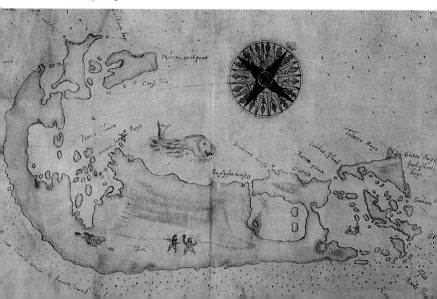

Sir George Somers

1543, which is now called Spanish Rock in the Spittal Pond Nature Reserve, indicates that at least the occasional soul was washed ashore, but apparently none chose to remain in this hostile place and set up a permanent home.

In 1593, Henry May had the dubious distinction of becoming the first Englishman known to be shipwrecked here. He was hitching a northbound ride home from the Caribbean with the French Captain de la Barbotièr, reputedly a pirate, when they had the misfortune to run aground on the notorious reefs. According to Henry May, the crew thought they had passed the dangerous area and 'gave themselves up to carousing'. Unfortunately, the relieved sailors started their celebrations too soon, and the ship eventually ran aground.

On reaching shore they found that the island was an unbroken forest of cedar. The resourceful sailors built a new boat with cedar wood and tortoise oil and set sail for home. Back in London, May described his sojourn on these islands and kindled marginal interest in their future potential.

Early Settlers

Isolated and desolate, the Bermudas nevertheless remained uninhabited until the shipwreck of the vessel *Sea Venture*; the ship foundered off St George's Island in 1609 whilst en route to resupply the faltering colony of Jamestown, in Virginia. The dreadful storm which caused the wreck and which was graphically described by one of the passengers is believed to have given Shakespeare material for *The Tempest*. Sir George Somers, the admiral of that ill-fated relief fleet, is the accredited founder of Bermuda. Once again, the island's cedar forests provided the material to build ships which would take the stranded sailors home. The *Deliverance* and *Patience* set sail for Virginia the following year.

St George, early 1800s

Sir George's enthusiasm for the islands was undimmed, and subsequently resulted in the first settlers arriving in 1612. Somers never saw that historic event, however; he died during his second visit in 1610. His body was taken back to England but his heart was buried in what is now called Somers Garden in St George.

It was the enthusiasm of his son, Matthew, which inspired the establishment of the Somers Island Company, to which King James I granted a charter to govern the islands in accordance with English law. Thanks initially to a shipwreck, Bermuda became in time a British colony.

At first, the situation was pretty chaotic. The early colonists soon discovered how to distil liquor and the first governor, Richard Moore, a former ship's carpenter, had to contend with drunken, unruly behaviour. He was, however, responsible for the constitution of a church and several forts as defence against Spanish adventurers. He was succeeded by Daniel Tucker, a strict disciplinarian, then by Nathaniel Butler (1619–22), who brought order to the islands and increased the production of tobacco which had been planted by the first settlers and for a while was used as currency.

By 1622, Governor Butler's records show that the population had risen to about 1500; within another 10 years, this figure had doubled. The majority of the arrivals were from England, although a steady influx of slaves gradually altered the balance. Statistics show that by 1699, roughly 25 percent of the population was of African origin. By 1749, this had climbed to 55 percent; and in 1833 (the year before emancipation), the population consisted of 4,279 whites and 3,612 slaves. The workforce was supplemented with rebellious Irishmen, as well as Scottish Highlanders captured during the 18th-century Jacobean disturbances. North American Indian prisoners were brought here in the earlier decades, and many present-day residents of St David's Island proudly bear the features of their incarcerated ancestors.

Proud mother, c1895

A Nation of Shipbuilders

The American War of Independence put Bermuda in a difficult position. Their economy was dependent on ties with the United States and the people, being colonials themselves, must have shared some of the Americans' grievances. But officially the islands were loyal to the Crown and if any Bermudians were involved in the removal, at George Washington's request, of 100 barrels of gunpowder from Bermuda's powder magazine, it was never proved. Governor Bruere called it 'a heinous and atrocious crime' but found no one to punish for it. American prisoners were housed on the island, which may have contributed to the despatch of an American invasion fleet in 1779. They were beaten back by British reinforcements but the act made Britain realise that Bermuda's defences needed strengthening. In the 1820s a penal colony was established to help in the construction of the Royal Naval Dockyard.

Historically, Bermudians have always been closely connected with seafaring. Their boat-building industry, based on the local cedar which made light fast ships, took off in the late 17th century. Countless numbers of Bermudians have gone to sea, often as captains of their own vessels; many never returned. They have gained reputations as whalers, fishermen and quite a few, such as the notorious Hezekiah Frith, became privateers – the polite nomenclature for a legalised pirate – and made healthy profits. Local shipbuilders produced the revolutionary design of the Bermuda fitted dinghy, a unique sailing craft which is only ever raced in these waters.

During the 19th century, Bermuda played a vital commercial role in the American Civil War (1861–65). Vessels from both sides made their way into her ports – St George for preference; guns and ammunition were the prized bargaining commodity which the islands had to offer these eager customers and which made many

Bermuda Dinghy, c1900

merchants very rich indeed. When the war ended, and the profitable trade was no more, Bermuda's economy suffered badly, particularly as new technological advances made their wooded boat-building industry redundant, and their supplies of cedar were sorely depleted.

It was a difficult time, but Bermuda successfully made the transition to agriculture and soon became a market garden for the rapidly growing city of New York. Because of the mild climate, all manner of vegetables, both exotic and basic, were grown here throughout the year and exported to the US mainland. The success of this enterprise was partly due to the skills and experience of an

Banana Tree and Fruit - Bermuda

influx of industrious Azorean farm workers who began to settle here in 1850. The popularity of Bermuda's onions reached such proportions that to this day islanders still proudly refer to themselves as 'onions'. (The demise of that specific branch of local trade, by the way, was due to a devious American opportunist who secured some of the onion seeds, took them back to Texas, renamed his farm 'Bermuda' and promptly marketed 'Bermuda Onions'.)

The First Tourists

With the gradual decline of an agriculturally-based economy throughout the early part of the 20th century, tourism was developed as the front running money-earner. With the encouragement and financial support of the Furness Withy Shipping Company, who offered to supply regular passenger arrivals, hotels were built at Castle Harbour and Mid Ocean, each with an attractive golf course. In these early stages, interestingly enough, Bermuda was seen as a winter resort, attracting a substantial number of regular guests from the eastern seaboard of the United States, seeking to escape the cold, severe weather of the mainland.

Princess Louise, a daughter of Queen Victoria, was one of the earliest tourists and where a princess went for her holidays others were inclined to follow. Among them was author Mark Twain, who exclaimed in 1910 that whilst others might continue looking for Paradise, he'd prefer to remain in Bermuda. American painter Winslow Homer also visited, as did British writer Rudyard Kipling and large numbers of anonymous but well-heeled sun-seekers.

The development of tourism was disrupted by the outbreak of World War I, but picked up again when peace returned. By 1931, an end-to-end railway system had become operational, enabling visitors to see and enjoy the scenic beauty

Bermuda

of the whole island, whilst facilitating the travel of Bermudians going about their everyday affairs. Farmers used the train to carry produce to market and to collect supplies and equipment from the docks. (Uneconomical to operate and maintain, however, it was dismantled in 1948 and sold to Guyana.)

Bermudian Bases

During World War II, as part of the so-called 'Destroyer Deal', Winston Churchill negotiated and signed a 99-year wartime landlease with the American government. This treaty, signed in 1941, led to the building of a US military base on part

Trains and boats

of St David's Island. Although built for strategic purposes the airstrip greatly facilitated arrivals and departures among visitors and residents alike. Bulk cargo, however, continues to arrive by sea.

The establishment of a US military base in Bermuda at this time only served to augment Bermuda's strategic value. The British Navy had always used the islands as a focal point of their Atlantic and Caribbean operations (it still does). American forces stationed on the islands increased after the invasion of Pearl Harbor, and Bermuda was surrounded by German U-boats.

The islands were never invaded – although the offensive cut off vital supplies. The legendary chase of the German vessel *Graf Spee* was partly orchestrated from here, and the wartime British censors established an intelligence-gatheringstation in Bermuda. (At the time of the momentous Cuban Missile Crisis of 1962, President Kennedy was to receive much of his intelligence from aircraft operating from this small Bermuda airfield.)

Throughout the post-World War II era, the Bermudian economy has grown steadily and healthily: the number of visitors continues to rise; the shipping register attracts more and more vessels; the overseas business community and banking services continue to expand. Landmark changes have also occurred in the law, with legislation which has sought to provide worker protection, ensure universal suffrage and safeguard the civil rights of all Bermudians.

Black Bermudians first became a significant political force in the late 1950s and in 1971 Sir Edward Richards became the island's first black government leader. Since the Constitutional Conference of 1968, Bermuda has been a self-governing, self-regulating colony, entirely responsible for its own affairs in all areas except for internal security and external defence.

St George

God's Country

Justifiably renowned as a peaceful and stable island, Bermuda was rocked, in 1973, by the assassination of its governor, Sir Richard Sharples, and his aide de camp, by a small group of extremists. All social groups were stunned by such an unprecedented incident. It remains an exceptional scar on this country's traditional reputation for safety and non-violence.

Bermuda's usual good fortune in the face of hurricanes also took a turn for the worse in 1987, when Hurricane Emily scored a direct hit, inflicting considerable damage to property from one end of the island to the other. The historic walls around St George were damaged by the hurricane's force, as were the National Trust properties of Verdmont and Winterhaven. Commenting on the near miraculous absence of personal injury, Premier Sir John Swan expressed no surprise and calmly remarked that Bermuda was indeed God's country.

Seeing the sights

At the present time, Bermuda remains a haven for tourists, offering them scenic beauty and a tranquil refuge from the faster pace of many contemporary life-styles. The flourishing tourist industry is carefully managed to ensure that Bermuda's quality of life is maintained. Additionally, it has developed into a major international business centre, with thousands of offshore companies taking advantage of special tax exemption privileges and an ultra-modern network of telecommunications.

Historical Highlights

1503 Discovery of the islands by Juan de Bermudez.

1543 Inscription carved at Spanish Rock confirms existence of early shipwreck survivor.

1593 Shipwreck of Henry May provides earliest description for English government.

1609 Shipwreck of Sir George Somers and passengers aboard *Sea Venture*, whilst bound for Virginia, marks the beginning of a permanent settlement.

1612 Arrival of first colonists from England aboard *The Plough*. Under first governor, former ship's carpenter Richard Moore, they settled mainly on St George Island.

1615 Somers Island Company is formed to undertake responsibility for colony's development.

1616 First Assizes, first Indians and Negroes arrive.

1617 Richard Norwood completes first island survey.

1620 State House and first jail built.

1651 Witchcraft trial of Jeanne Gardiner – executed in St George.

1684 Somers Island Company dissolved and the legal status of colony reassessed.

1712 St Peter's Church partially destroyed by storm, but rebuilt within a year.

1722 Government House built on a hillside overlooking St George.

1731 Serious outbreak of Yellow Fever.

1775 Bermudian involvement in 'The Gunpowder Scandal', which gives support to American colonists during War of Independence.

1784 Joseph Stockdale establishes first newspaper press.

1790 Legislation passed to build a town to be called Hamilton.

1809 Construction work commences on Royal Naval Dockyard.

1815 Bermuda's capital changes from St George to Hamilton.

1824 Convict labour arrives from Britain to help with construction of Royal Naval Dockyard.

1834 Emancipation of slaves.

1846 Gibb's Hill Lighthouse built, to designs of William Facy.

1861 American Civil War sees Bermuda commercially active on both sides.

1871 Causeway opened, forging road link between East End and Hamilton.

1879 St David's Lighthouse built.

1887 First telephone link between St George and Hamilton.

1901 South African Boer prisoners arrive in Bermuda.

1902 First Somerset-St George cricket 'Cup Match' is held.

1906 First Newport-Bermuda yacht race is organised.

1915 Initial contingent of Bermuda Volunteer Rifle Corps heads off to World War I.

1920 300th anniversary of parliament is celebrated.

1931 Bermuda Railway commences island-wide service.

1940 British wartime censorship station established.

1941 US government starts to build bases and airport.

1946 Introduction of motor cars.

1951 'Extinct' cahow bird is discovered in Bermuda.

1958 Wreck of the *Sea Venture* is discovered.

1961 Anti-discrimination legislation is passed.

1968 Constitutional Conference establishes Bermuda's self-governing colony status.

1971 Sir Edward Richards becomes first black Premier.

1983 Bermuda becomes a British Dependent Territory.

1985 An original Perot Stamp, Bermuda's first, sells for nearly $60,000.

1987 Tourism figures reach unprecedented annual high, exceeding 600,000 visitors.

Hamilton

A day-long itinerary which takes in a walk around the shopping streets of Hamilton, a visit to the Bermuda National Gallery in the City Hall, the Anglican Cathedral, and Fort Hamilton with its magnificent views plus an international choice of restaurants for dinner.

In 1790, legislation was passed to build the town of Hamilton. It became the capital of Bermuda in 1815 and was incorporated as a city in 1897. Among the many reasons for transferring this role from the original capital of St George were Hamilton's central location and considerably larger harbour. The city continues to be the social and economic hub of the country. The narrow streets

Hamilton waterfront

beyond the harbour teem with shoppers and office workers and there is a busy, urban ambience. The city has a population of only 2,000 people but because it blends seamlessly into its parish, Pembroke, it seems larger than it really is.

Hamilton's setting is quite spectacular and offers countless opportunities not just to experience the hustle and bustle of city life, but also to enjoy tranquil vistas over the water. The principal thoroughfare is **Front Street**, which stretches all the way along the waterfront from Albouy's Point, past the cruise-ship terminals and freight sheds, until it eventually becomes East Broadway and ends at the roundabout at Foot-of-the-Lane. In the opposite direction, it becomes Pitts Bay Road and heads towards Spanish Point. Front Street – aptly named because it follows the harbour front – is lined with a tempting succession of shops, each selling wares chosen from the world's finest markets. Customers can purchase cameras, watches, jewellery, designer fashions, Scottish kilts, Wedgwood, Royal Doulton china, and everything from Persian carpets to tee-shirts.

For this reason I recommend you spend your first morning in Bermuda shopping or just strolling around. The **Windjammer Gallery**, on Front Street, has a great variety of local and imported prints and original artwork; **Pegasus**, along Pitts Bay Road, has Bermuda's finest collection of authentic maps and antique prints; **Heritage House**, also along Pitts Bay Road, sells antiques

Front Street

and local art. The next parallel road up from Front Street is Reid Street; then comes Church Street; then Victoria Street. These and the connecting streets, lanes and malls, especially **Washington Mall**, are all excellent spots for the shopper.

This may be the customarily recognised shopping area – 'downtown' so to speak – but you should not feel restricted. Explore the roads beyond this nucleus and all sorts of unexpected pleasures can be found. For those hoping to acquire less traditional gifts and

Perot Post Office

clothing, a stroll through the back-of-town area of **Court Street**, for example, will reveal a great variety of shops for those looking for more unusual goods.

But Hamilton is far more than just a venue for spending money in stores, restaurants and bars. It is filled with history, with restful parks, relaxing water views, art galleries and a fort overlooking everything. At the first available opportunity you should send your postcards from the original little post office in which Postmaster William Perot used to sit 150 years ago, patiently hand-stamping and signing Bermuda's first mail (**Perot Post Office** on Queen Street). The office feels authentic, from the brass candlesticks to the wooden counter and it is great fun to sit at one of the old-fashioned desks, perched on a tall wooden stool, writing a postcard.

Adjacent to the Perot Post Office, is the **Main Lending Library** (Monday to Friday 9.30am–5pm), housed in a delightful old building on the edge of **Par-la-Ville Gardens**, and well worth an early stop. This used to be the home of William Perot and he was responsible for planting the now massive **rubber tree** which stands in front of the building and offers shade in the heat of the day. The library contains reference and lending sections, as well as a rare book room. A wide verandah provides perfect shade in which

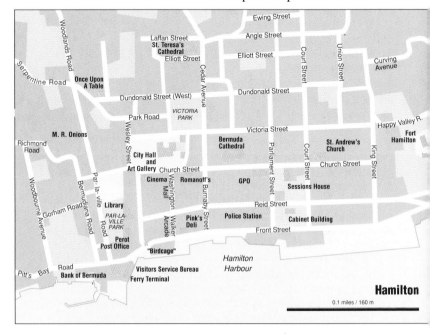

Hamilton

0.1 miles / 160 m

to sit, read or watch passersby. Inside the main entrance, there is a small display of Bermudian memorabilia – including a portrait of Sir George Somers, whose ship, the *Sea Venture*, was shipwrecked off the coast of what is now St George's Island, in 1609.

The sea chest and lodestone belonging to Sir George, the founder of Bermuda, are also here, although his heart lies in Somers' Gardens, St George (*see Day 2 Itinerary*). On the wall near the door is the mould of a rock carving known as Spanish Rock, which is thought to have been made by a shipwrecked Portuguese sailor in 1543. Off the

Library verandah

lobby is the charming **Historical Society Museum**, two rooms filled with history – and an accommodating, well-informed guide ready to answer questions.

The gardens outside the library are carefully arranged with pathways to wind you through the flower beds, bushes and trees which decorate the lawns. It's a pleasant place for a picnic or a stroll after visiting the library. There is another, smaller park at **Albouy's Point**, just off Front Street behind the Bank of Bermuda building; it directly overlooks the harbour and is an ideal spot from which to watch a variety of yachts, ships and ferries coming and going.

After a hectic morning's shopping, or simply exploring the busy streets, stop for a quick lunch before the afternoon's activities. Try the small delicatessen named **Pinks**, on **The Walkway**, which links Front and Reid streets. Pinks serves wonderful coffee and makes some of the island's best, and most healthy, sandwiches. Alternatively, get something hot from The Flying Chef Beergarden, off **Washington Lane**, by the shopping mall; the service is fast and they have many different hot dishes. Or if you are really in a hurry, get a hot beef pie and coffee from Degraffs lunch wagon, which is always parked in the far corner of the City Hall car park. After lunch, we'll be off again.

Hamilton City Hall (Monday to Friday 9am–5pm), is on **Church Street**, two blocks inland from the harbour, and is an imposing white structure dominated by a weather-vaned tower. (Immediately adjacent to the City Hall is

Hitching a ride

Inside City Hall

Hamilton's bus terminal, so it is easy to find.) In addition to being the administrative hub of Hamilton, the City Hall also accommodates two interesting art galleries, a theatre, a lobby filled with portraits of previous mayors, and various corporation offices.

The two art galleries are upstairs. Climb the stairs to the uppermost gallery, the permanent home of the Bermuda Society of Arts. Exhibitions of members' work are ongoing throughout the year – interrupted only by the annual show, or special feature displays. The **Bermuda National Gallery** (Monday to Saturday 10am–4pm, Sunday 12.30–4pm) is on the next level down. This was established fairly recently, so that the people of Bermuda and visitors would have somewhere to view and enjoy international and local artwork in a climate-controlled environment.

Exhibitions are arranged from the permanent collection, as well as from works of art loaned locally or imported for the occasion. Exhibitions are frequently arranged in conjunction with 'Masterworks', a local foundation whose sole purpose is to acquire and repatriate Bermuda paintings from overseas.

Downstairs, off the main entrance to City Hall, there is usually a small philatelic display arranged according to a specific theme or era. At the opposite end of the hall is the **theatre**. Local amateur productions are presented here, but this is also a prime venue for participants in the Bermuda Festival – a winter entertainment extravaganza (January to March) which attracts an international programme of professional performers in an arts feast of dance, song, music, comedy, magic and theatre.

Just behind the City Hall is another secluded park – **Victoria Park**, dominated by a genuine 19th-century gazebo-like bandstand. When Bermuda hosted a military garrison, regimental bands performed here on a regular basis; individual performances are still arranged by the town corporation throughout the year.

If you come out of the City Hall and walk to your left, up along Church Street, you will come to Hamilton's **Anglican Cathedral**, a few blocks away. (The Catholic Cathedral, St Theresa's is up Cedar Avenue, in the other direction; the main Muslim mosque is right next door.) In keeping with tradition, the cathedral is built in Gothic style – resplendent with tower, belfry, bells, buttresses and decorated pinnacles. The interior is lined with characteristic arches, cloisters and commemorative tablets, and there is a magnificent organ and an imposing altar area. The stone figures located along the rear wall were created by the late Byllee Lang, who is recognised as one of Bermuda's finest sculptors.

Leave the cathedral through the front portals and turn left along Church Street. At the very end (just a couple of blocks) you will see a small sign directing you up to **Fort Hamilton** (Monday to Friday 9.30am–5pm). It is only about a 10-minute walk from the cathedral and the view from the ramparts is more than worthwhile, even on a hot, humid summer day. It was constructed, like so many of the other fortifications around these islands, during the 19th century, and symbolised the continuing expansion of the British Empire.

The fort commands a magnificent view along the entire length of Hamilton Harbour, and affords a spectacular panorama of the islands and bays, all of the city itself, and the entire western end of Bermuda. There is a well-tended moat, with a pathway meandering among dense, tropical vegetation – and lots of passageways and empty munitions rooms to explore. But the view alone is worth the visit.

Freedom on two wheels

For those who have hired a bike (*see Practical Information*, page 79) there is one quick additional option for a seven minute side-trip and a swim. Take a ride along Front Street and carry on to its natural continuation, Pitts Bay Road. Keep on going, following signs to **Spanish Point**. Here, there is a beachside park and popular swimming spot. The wreck just off the shoreline is the remnant of the 19th-century **Floating Dock**, formerly anchored at the Dockyard; it is now a haven for fish and marine life and makes an attractive area for snorkelling.

Anglican Cathedral

DAY 2

St George

Experience the island's historical and cultural origins by taking a stroll through Old St George, starting at Ordnance Island and visiting the old buildings and museums in King's Square and Water Street. Buses go to St George's on a regular basis from all parts of the island. Special boat charters also visit here from Hamilton. By motor scooter, it takes about 20 minutes from Flatts, 45 minutes from Hamilton and approximately 1½ hours from Somerset. Be sure to book a table for dinner at the Carriage House, tel: 297 1270 or the Margaret Rose, tel: 297 1301.

It doesn't matter whether or not you've been to these islands before: any visit to Bermuda should always include a trip to **St George**. This wonderful old town not only helps to set the tone and mood of the entire country, it also helps to put everything else you see during your stay into some sort of historical perspective.

George Somers' statue

Whether arriving by bus, boat, taxi or rented motor scooter, sooner or later everyone inevitably gravitates towards the Town Square, so it's natural that a tour of St George should begin right here. Actually, not quite in King's Square itself, but on **Ordnance Island**, which lies a few yards away on the other side of a small bridge.

Ordnance Island is dominated by two distinctive structures: one is the imposing statue of Bermuda's accredited founder, Sir George Somers; the other is the replica of a 17th-century ship named *Deliverance*. Between them they represent Bermuda's earliest human habitation.

Sir George was the admiral of a small fleet sent by the

'Deliverance'

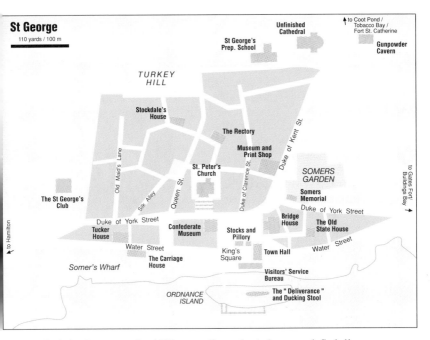

St George

110 yards / 100 m

TURKEY HILL

Unfinished Cathedral

St George's Prep. School

to Coot Pond / Tobacco Bay / Fort St. Catherine

Gunpowder Cavern

Stockdale's House

The Rectory

Museum and Print Shop

Duke of Kent St.

Old Maid's Lane

St. Peter's Church

Silk Alley

Queen St.

Duke of Clarence St.

SOMERS GARDEN

Somers Memorial

The St George's Club

Duke of York Street

Tucker House

Confederate Museum

Stocks and Pillory

Bridge House

Duke of York Street

The Old State House

to Gates Fort / Buildings Bay

to Hamilton

Water Street

The Carriage House

King's Square

Town Hall

Water Street

Somer's Wharf

Visitors' Service Bureau

ORDNANCE ISLAND

The "Deliverance" and Ducking Stool

Virginia Company, in 1609, to relieve the beleaguered fledgling American colony of Jamestown. Battered and fragmented by a tempestuous mid-Atlantic storm, the fleet scattered and Sir George, aboard the *Sea Venture*, was shipwrecked off the northern coast of the island which now bears his name. Remarkably enough, except for some wild hogs and an abundance of birds, turtles and fish, they found 'Las Bermudas' to be completely uninhabited.

During the next 10 months, the 150 or so survivors worked diligently to make the two boats which would prove to be their eventual salvation: *Patience* and *Deliverance*. Once launched, the passengers and crew continued their voyage to the North American mainland, leaving two men behind as the sole resident population of this cluster of coral islands, to claim them for the British Crown. Thus, Sir George Somers and *Deliverance* mark the cornerstone of Bermuda's history. The **ship's replica** is open to the public. The **statue of Somers** is by the talented Bermudian sculptor Desmond Fountain and depicts the admiral at the triumphant moment of exclaiming: 'Land ahoy!' (As a matter of interest, he is facing the precise spot where *Sea Venture* was wrecked, on the other side of St George's Island.)

Town crier

From here, you should cross back into **King's Square**, complete with **War Memorial**, a **19th-century cannon** and St George's **Town Hall**. Imagine, if you will, that when the first deliberate settlers (as opposed to shipwrecked mariners) arrived here in 1612 there were no buildings whatsoever and certainly no paved square. Instead, this spot was just a muddy inlet. It was around here, however, that the first Bermudians chose to build their houses,

27

carefully keeping all construction just above the high-water mark. Although none of those original wooden-thatched structures have survived, many of the oldest buildings in Bermuda are still found around the rim which rises about the present King's Square.

One of these is the **State House** (Wednesday only 10am–4pm), situated just off the right-hand corner, at the top of a rise paved with red bricks. This distinctive structure is a landmark within the town and is clearly visible from afar because of its square, turret-like appearance and white limestone walls. Started in approximately 1619, it took nearly three years to complete and was the first stone building. When finished, it became the focal point of the island's government for the next two centuries and for a while also served as a gunpowder magazine. It is currently rented by a local lodge whose members, each Easter, publicly pay a fee of just one peppercorn per annum to the Accountant General of Bermuda, during the colourful **Peppercorn Ceremony**.

In the vicinity of the old State House stand several other buildings of note. Among these, to the left looking up the 'red brick road', is **Bridge House** (Monday to Saturday 10am–5pm, Sunday in summer 11am–3pm), which is the oldest piece of domestic property in Bermuda still being used as a residence. (There are deeds transferring its ownership, dated 1697.) Like many other historic buildings in St George, Bridge House is presently owned and maintained by the Bermuda National Trust. It is now rented out as two separate private apartments, plus an art gallery and craft shop. By entering the latter, visitors can have a glimpse of what the original dining rooms and entrance hallway were like. Also adjacent to the State House are two outstanding examples of Bermudian architecture from the turn of the 18th century: **Buckingham** and **Reeve Court**.

Turn left at the State House and a narrow alleyway will lead you directly down into **Somers Gardens**. This delightful spot is a well-groomed park and home to a diverse selection of plants, trees, flowers and bushes – the majority of which have become naturalised to Bermuda, meaning that seeds, bulbs, cuttings and saplings which were transplanted here many centuries ago now thrive here as if this were their natural home.

1609 – 1909

IN COMMEMORATION OF THE SETTLEMENT OF THESE ISLANDS ON THE 28TH OF JULY 1609 AND IN HONOUR OF ADMIRAL SIR GEORGE SOMERS KT AT WHOSE INSTANCE LARGELY THE SETTLEMENT WAS EFFECTED THIS MEMORIAL HAS BEEN ERECTED OUT OF A GRANT MADE BY THE LEGISLATURE OF THIS COLONY

At the entrance to Somers Gardens is an **obelisk** commemorating the 300th anniversary of the wrecking of the *Sea Venture*. On a wall nearby is a **plaque** which somewhat gruesomely declares that 'near here was buried the heart of Sir George Somers'. It seems that the ill-fated admiral liked Bermuda and, after finally arriving at Jamestown, offered to make a quick about-turn in order to get some fresh food – fish, birds and eggs. But he died here soon after returning, in 1610, and made a deathbed request that his heart be buried in these enchanted isles, although his son, Matthew, took his body back to England.

If you take a stroll through the gardens and exit via the gateway on the other side, you will find yourself in the back streets of St George. It is among these narrow byways that you will truly be exposed to Bermuda as it used to be. Sufficiently wide to allow the passage of a horse and cart, the streets are filled with character, low walls and an abundance of overhanging plants. It requires very little imagination to propel oneself back into another era; into a lifestyle devoid of motorised traffic, when children chased hoops and rarely wore shoes. Banana plants appear from behind garden fences and nasturtiums trail their way among flowering hedges and wild geraniums. Pawpaws peer above Surinam cherry bushes and citrus trees; there are still the smells of home cooking and the sounds of school children at play.

Turn left at the rear gate of the park and wander a while. You can't get lost. If you make your way up any slope, you will probably emerge in the local 18-hole golf course. If you make your way downhill, you will be back at either King's Square, or alongside the waters of the harbour. Night or day, the backstreets of St George convey the real character of these islands – and offer countless delights for anyone with a camera, and an eye for winding lanes, shutters, shadows, rooftops and that more intangible quality called atmosphere.

White roofs and shutters

Sandwiches 'n' smiles

There are several good places for a lunchtime snack, and none of them are far away, so you won't have to retrace too many steps. You could buy a fish sandwich and cold drink from **Angeline's**, on York Street opposite the Somers Gardens, or sit under the balcony of the **Wharf Tavern** on Water Street, and enjoy one of their 'specials' with a glass of cold beer. **Moonglow**, also on Water Street, does excellent fish sandwiches. If you can find a spot on the verandah, it is entertaining to sit outside the **Pub on the Square** and watch the world go by, while enjoying a cold drink and one of their very tasty steak-and-kidney pies. (See also *Eating Out*.)

St Peter's Church

While exploring this unique town make sure you find a moment to enter **St Peter's Church**. A church has stood on this site since Bermuda's original colonisation. There is a persistent aroma from the cedar which was used in its construction, and the walls are lined with plaques and memorials describing events and personages from Bermuda's rich history. There is a magnificent organ, comfortable wooden pews, 17th-century silverware, and autographs of the Queen, President Kennedy and other visiting dignitaries.

In the 19th century there were plans to replace St Peter's with a neo-Gothic cathedral, but costs rose so steeply that the project was abandoned. The Unfinished Cathedral now soars towards the sky, its base surrounded by undergrowth and blocks of masonry, more famous and more photographed than if it had been completed.

There are many interesting places which should be visited in the Old Town, and the Visitors' Service Bureau on King's Square can provide maps and directions. Among the most important are two museums. The unusual **Carriage Museum** (Monday to Friday 10am–5pm), on Water Street, features a display of authentic carriages, primarily from the 19th century and is regarded by some as a monument to Bermuda's resistance to the motor car.

St George's Historical Society Museum (Monday to Friday 10am–4pm), is in Featherbed Alley, with furnishings and other household items arranged as though the house were still an occupied residence. In the basement is a working model of the original 15th-century Guttenburg Press which revolutionised communications. The **Confederate Museum** (April to October: Monday to Saturday 9.30am–4.30pm; November to March: Monday to Saturday 10am–4pm), on King's Square, highlights the town's intriguing association

Tucker House interior

with the Southern Confederate States during the American Civil War (1861–65), when it served as the home of Major Walker, the Confederacy's resident commercial agent. The **Tucker House** (April to October: Monday to Saturday 9.30am–4.30pm; November to March: Monday to Saturday 10am–4pm), on Water Street, is delightfully displayed as a living museum, with furnishings and decor exhibited in such a way as to reconstruct the atmosphere of daily life in the late 18th-century homestead of the Tucker family (*see* the excursion to National Trust Properties).

There is an excellent selection of shops and restaurants to satisfy all interests, tastes and pockets and, because of lower rents, prices are sometimes less expensive here than elsewhere on the island. There are some excellent buys in Icelandic sweaters from Constables, located beneath the Confederate Museum; **Somers' Wharf**, located on Water Street, is a small complex of diverse waterside stores; for locally made arts and crafts, a visit to The Bridge House Art Gallery is essential. General souvenirs and tee-shirts can be found at Watermelons, on Bridge Street, Another World, in King's Square by the Visitors' Service Bureau, and Paradise Gift Shop, also in the main square. Robertson's, opposite the Post Office, is the principal drug, gift and stationery store. If you are here on a Wednesday you might see a demonstration of the ducking stool, once used to punish petty offenders and nagging wives.

Round off your day with dinner at the **Carriage House Restaurant**, Water Street, tel: 297 1270 or at the **Margaret Rose**, in St George's Club, Rose Hill, tel: 297 1301, where, ideally, you will have booked a table earlier in the day. The food at both places is exceptionally good and the Margaret Rose also boasts magnificent harbour views.

Ducking stool

Dockyard and the West End

A trip around the Royal Naval Dockyard and Bermuda's West End, combined with visits to Somerset Village and Mangrove Bay, ending up at the Royal Naval Cemetery. By road, it takes about 45 minutes to reach Hamilton, by ferry, about 40 minutes. Both buses and ferries make regular trips. Book a table for your evening meal at Tio Pepe, tel: 238 1897 or the Waterlot Inn, tel: 238 0510 in Southampton, or go back to Hamilton for dinner.

Dockyard

Visitors wishing to tour the western end of Bermuda have the option of travelling by road or ferry. The ideal way to do it, however, is a combination of both: take the ferry up, and return along the South Shore by bus or bike (or vice-versa). If you decide on dinner in Southampton (and have brought semi-smart clothes) treat yourself to a taxi back to Hamilton. The West End includes the region which extends from Somerset Village out to Dockyard.

Dockyard was formerly a major servicing station for the Royal Navy; British vessels of the 19th century would come here for repairs, fuel and provisions and to allow their weathered sailors a chance to relax. Construction began in 1809 and by the time it was nearing completion, 70 years later, it had become a self-supporting naval facility. The fleet that attacked Washington DC in 1814 sailed from here. The British Navy retains a considerably smaller presence today, due to modern technology and communications, but land-based HMS *Malabar* remains a vital link in the Western Atlantic.

Today, the buildings which once housed military personnel, and where they kept supplies, repaired masts, sewed sails and made storage barrels, have adopted different identities. Since 1975, the entire complex has been redeveloped for commercial and recreational purposes. Where once there was a guarded keep and munitions

Exhibit in Maritime Museum

centre, there is now a Maritime Museum; where once the air sizzled with heat from a cooper's forge, there is now a craft market and pub; a warehouse has become a factory for the Island Pottery company.

The ferry ride from Hamilton takes approximately 40 minutes and, depending on its route, may well make scheduled stops at **Somerset Bridge**, **Cavello Bay**, **Boaz Island** and **Watford Bridge**. It is a delightful ride among the islands and bays of Hamilton Harbour and the **Great Sound**, which is the basin formed by the left 'hook' of Bermuda. Many of the islands in The Sound are named after birds and animals: Goat, Cat, Goose and Partridge islands being a few of them. Passengers may alight at any of these stages, but it makes for more convenient touring to disembark at Dockyard itself. Bikes are permitted on board the ferries, which berth at the quay alongside an international yachting marina. The road on your right will take you to the Maritime Museum, the Bermuda Arts Centre and the Craft Market.

The **Maritime Museum** (daily 10am–4.30pm) was opened by Queen Elizabeth II in 1975, although the building itself was finished more than a century earlier, in 1857. Here visitors will find all manner of displays highlighting the inseparable ties which these islands have always had with the sea. Passing from building to building, Bermuda's maritime history is explained; the exhibits themselves: ships, costumes, memorabilia, badges, signs, logbooks, paintings, etchings, maps and photographs provide a guided tour of a shipping era which, of course, has never really ended.

Particularly interesting exhibits are the **Boat Loft**, focusing on locally built

34

craft and restoration techniques currently being employed on donated derelicts; the **Bromby Collection** of old bottles, the most comprehensive in Bermuda, and the **Treasure House** – offering an insight into divingmethods over the centuries, wreck locations and samples of treasure retrieved from the ocean bed.

Jaqui Murray Hall

In the grounds outside, you can wander among the ramparts. Look at cannons, think of frigates and gaze with wonder upon the extravagant splendour of **Commissioner's House**, commanding an uninterrupted view from high on a slope above the keepyard. It is said that its Welsh slate roof, the marble fireplace and mahogany woodwork were shipped here from the United Kingdom. Of all the postings which a Victorian officer might have received, this was surely the most sought-after in the British Empire.

Directly opposite the entrance to the Maritime Museum is the **Bermuda Arts Centre** (Tuesday to Saturday 10am–4pm, Sunday noon–5pm), formally opened by Princess Margaret in 1984. This gallery contains regularly changing exhibitions of local and overseas artwork, most of which is for sale. There is a good selection of Bermudian prints and notelets. There are three working studios in this building: in one, painter Jaqui Murray Hall can usually be seen; in another, quiltmaker Lynn Morrell's colourful work is displayed; wood sculptor Chesley Trott is invariably in his studio.

Next door, held in what was once the cooperage of this naval establishment, is the **Craft Market**, and now it is the smell of cedar wood rather than beer

The West End

1 mile / 1.6 km

Royal Naval Dockyard
Maritime Museum
Cinema
IRELAND ISLAND NORTH
IRELAND ISLAND SOUTH
Black Bay
Malabar Rd
Grassy Bay
Long Bay
Mangrove Bay
BOAZ ISLAND
Somerset
Watford Bridge
Bus Stop
Post Office
Ferry Shop
SOMERSET ISLAND
Visitors Service Bureau (seasonal)
Cavello Bay
Great Sound
Scaur Hill Fort
Ely's Harbour
Somerset Rd
Somerset Bridge
Middle Rd

which fills the air. Seeking to recapture the genuine atmosphere of a craftsman's market, individual stalls, benches and tables are arranged informally about the hall, and visitors will always catch several of the artisans practising their craft. Jewellery and candlemaking, cedar work, stained glass and painting are just a few of the arts and crafts which are regularly demonstrated here.

On the other side of the ship's basin stands the long and distinctive **Clocktower Building**. Completed in 1857, the twin towers stand 100ft (30m) high and contain two English clocks: one telling the present time, the other giving the time of the next high tide. Originally used as the administrative and storage centre of the complex, the building has been converted into a mini shopping mall. Among the more unusual shops inside are Turkish Delights, featuring unusual fashions from Turkey; Michael Swan's small air-brushing studio; Ships Inn, selling books, including many secondhand titles; International Flags and Uniform Shop with its worldwide selection of nautical

memorabilia; Admiral's Locker, also selling nautical items; and Pina, with an array of casual wear, all locally designed and handpainted. Most of the shops are open every day. La Brioche serves wonderful coffee and, as its name suggests, has a good selection of fresh pastries.

Upstairs in the Clocktower Building, be sure to see the famous triptych by the renowned British painter Sam Morse-Brown, a longtime resident of Bermuda. The centrepiece of this trio of evocative pictures was completed whilst he still lived in England and eerily depicts man's potential future in the aftermath of a nuclear war. Originally, the triptych was exhibited in London's Southwark Cathedral, but the entire grouping is now permanently housed in Bermuda at the artist's request.

Mangrove Bay

If you didn't have too many pastries in La Brioche, and are now ready for lunch, there are several places to eat in the vicinity of Dockyard. The Frog and Onion Pub, opposite the Maritime Museum, offers typical pub fare and a plentiful choice of drinks. The New Freeport Gardens Restaurant is another good choice. It is quite informal and has an extensive menu; pizzas are recommended, as are fish dishes and steak sandwiches. Alternatively, there are some excellent places to eat at the next port of call, **Somerset Village**. In particular, both the Loyalty Inn and the Country Squire offer good food in attractive waterside settings.

The road from this part of Bermuda's West End leads directly into Somerset Village. Hugging the northern shore of the bay, this is a neat little hamlet, and a good place to buy souvenirs. For swimmers and beachcombers, the idyllic sweep of **Mangrove Bay** is delightful. Complete with a rim of swaying palms, it is quite shallow and therefore excellent for waders and safe for paddlers. The more adventurous can hire sailing boats, kayaks and snorkelling equipment. A few minutes around the corner from here, just off Cambridge Road, is another public beach, called **Long Bay**. It is a picturesque stretch of beach, and very popular with local swimmers because the water is deeper and it has fewer boat moorings than Mangrove Bay.

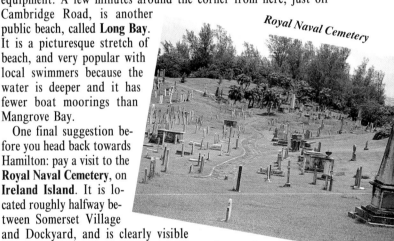

Royal Naval Cemetery

One final suggestion before you head back towards Hamilton: pay a visit to the **Royal Naval Cemetery**, on **Ireland Island**. It is located roughly halfway between Somerset Village and Dockyard, and is clearly visible from the main road. As the name indicates, it contains the graves of seamen and their families who have died in or near Bermuda since the Royal Navy commenced the operation of this Atlantic station, almost two centuries ago.

The cemetery is not only an interesting source of unusual information, but also contains some moving poetry. The headstones reveal much about the lives of those buried here; causes of death describe accidents and epidemics of yellow fever, infant mortality and drownings. Collectively, the graves offer an unusual insight into the social conditions of that bygone era which did so much to develop the West End of Bermuda.

After these sobering thoughts and the day's exertions, relax in the elegant bayside surroundings of the **Waterlot Inn**, enjoy some good Italian food at **Tio Pepe**, or choose one of Hamilton's restaurants when you get back to town.

1. The Railway Trails

Attractive walks along Bermuda's restored railway trails; each walk can take from half an hour to three hours, depending on how far you want to go. Wear comfortable shoes and take a hat for when the sun gets hot.

If you enjoy walking, the best time of the day is the morning. By midday the sun is well up and, in this humidity, even strolling in the shade can become arduous. Therefore, make an early start and go for a pleasant amble.

Some of the better walks are along the old Bermuda railway right-of-way. Here the pace is entirely unrushed, uncrowded and considerably safer than the country roads, most of which have no pavements. The Bermuda Ministry of Tourism publishes a free guide to the trails which shows access points for people arriving by bus.

Because the railway ran the full length of the island, there are sections to be found almost everywhere. Because home owners did not want the railway in their own back yards, the tracks were built near the shore and some 10 percent of them elevated on bridges, with the result that much of the trails offer spectacular views. In the 1980s the Bermuda government realised the value of these often gladed areas and undertook to clear overgrown vegetation and remove an accumulation of obstacles. The result is many miles of pathways for the public to wander along. There are also designated spots where novices can gain experience on the mopeds they have just rented – but this shouldn't spoil your pleasure.

One of the most picturesque trail walks starts at the **South Shore** roundabout, just outside Hamilton. Head westwards on that road, the entrance to the right-of-way being a few hundred yards up on the right-hand side of the present road. It follows a tunnel beneath the road and continues as a disused railway cutting. Within a matter of minutes, you are

Railway trail

walking among cultivated fields and through narrow pathways, flanked by trees and bushes. In season, many of these bushes are laden with Surinam cherries – an acquired taste for those more familiar with shiny tropical fruits, but a tasty delicacy to feast upon and whose calories you will soon walk off.

This particular stretch offers an elevated view over **Paget Marsh**, before it crosses the main road near **Horizons**. It then continues as a concealed pathway, meandering along fields and the backs of private gardens. Most of the route is protected by high shrubs and natural woods. With a few exceptions where it cuts across public roads, this section can be walked well beyond Belmont Golf Course, where trees conceal the Warwick Pond Bird Sanctuary, and deep into **Warwick Parish**; for much of the way, you will be oblivious to the rest of the world.

There is another splendid stretch to be walked just on the borders of **Southampton** and **Sandys parishes**. A convenient joining point might well be in the vicinity of Lantana, from which you could wander either eastwards or westwards and experience the same degree of pleasure. This is as charming a place to commence as any because of the presence of an old railway cutting and an attractive rustic bridge which crosses over the top. There are trees all about and the feeling is that of a glade – all most picturesque.

If you opt to go westwards, towards Somerset, you will find that most of the route is a fairly wide roadway which offers

Bucolic resident

excellent vistas out towards **Grassy Bay**, Dockyard and across some of the **smaller islands** of Hamilton Harbour. If you choose to head eastwards you will find yourself strolling among well-sheltered pathways which meander towards and around little inlets. Eventually, the western portion of the trail ends in a bus turnaround and car park which was originally the Somerset railway terminal.

By contrast, in **St George's Parish**, at Bermuda's East End, the railway trail along **Ferry Reach** presents walkers with the chance to stroll largely along the North Shore and have uninterrupted views of the ocean. If you decide to take this walk you may join the trail at Ferry Reach, just by the large

Ferry Point

Shell storage tanks. There is a small road on the right and the trail is clearly indicated down there and to the left. Initially, the descent is sudden and rather rugged, but once beyond this steep embankment the path opens up and becomes clear and flat. After a few minutes, you will come to the remnants of the West India Oil Docks Station; made out of natural Bermuda limestone blocks, it is typical of such stations in both size and shape. The still-used jetty can be seen extending offshore.

This section of railway trail mainly offers an unshaded walk along the coastline; however, it does pass **Lovers Lake** with its encircling park. A particularly unusual feature is the overhead flight-path of Bermuda's air traffic – so be prepared for the sights and sounds of low-flying aircraft. Further along, you will pass a 19th-century military cemetery, the beach at Whalebone Bay and then end at a Martello tower built in 1823.

2. Explore Bailey's Bay

A morning visit to a perfumery, a glass-blowing factory and the Leamington and Crystal caves. It takes about 35 minutes from Hamilton by bus or bike.

The area which Bermudians refer to as Bailey's Bay is not so much a watery cove, as the name may suggest, but rather the junction of two roads midway between St George and Flatts Village. At this point, where North Shore and Wilkinson Avenue intersect, a small community has grown up.

Bailey's Bay can be reached from Hamilton by bike or bus. If travelling by bus, ask to be put off at the **Swizzle Inn** – a necessary stop to quench your thirst on a hot day, although it might be a little early to sample their famous rum swizzle.

From this junction, you have ready access to three attractions: the Bermuda Perfumery, the Bermuda Glass Blowing Studio and two major caves – Leamington and Crystal.

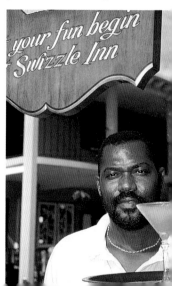

Swizzle tipple

The **Bermuda Perfumery** (Monday to Saturday 9am–5pm, Sunday 10am–4pm) is located just to the west, along the North Shore Road. Although this is a factory there are no extensive brick buildings or countless smoking chimneys. The perfumery is located in a large house, set amidst colourful sprawling gardens, in which most of the flowers which are used to make perfume are grown. They include jasmine, oleander, frangipani and Easter lily – the first of the flowers to be cultivated here.

Perfumery gardens

The perfumery began on a modest scale – in fact, it was housed in a wooden shed – in 1929 and two years later the proprietors acquired the 200-year-old farmhouse which became the business's new home. The factory portion of the estate is beneath the house and guided tours are conducted on an on-going, regular basis. You will be shown how the various fragrances are extracted from the blooms themselves and how these in turn are captured and transformed into recognisable perfumes. Each tour lasts perhaps 15 minutes and concludes inside the shop where bottles of the exotic perfumes may be sampled and purchased. Also, feel free to wander among the gardens and enjoy their sweet-smelling air. A charming little nature trail has been laid out here but it can be quite muddy so wear appropriate shoes.

From the perfumery, walk back to the Swizzle Inn and continue down Blue Hole hill. On the right you will come to the **Glass Blowing Studio**. If you have never watched this ancient craft being practised, then this is the perfect place to get an initiation because the floor plan has been designed so that visitors may sit and watch the artists at work, as well as purchase their wares.

The temperatures are inevitably very hot, reaching well over 110°F (43°C) in the work area, and if you look into the constantly open furnaces you will feel even hotter. There are three furnaces, each of which plays a key role in the manufacturing process. Because hot liquid glass is a dangerous commodity, the sequences involved in melting, blowing, shaping and detaching the finished article require expert coordination. It is fascinating to watch the complete understanding that has evolved between artist and apprentice. The work is done speedily and deliberately; sometimes just a short puff and a whirl before the glass is again plunged back into the glowing inferno of the furnace. This is Bermuda's first and only glass blowing studio. All items have been made and designed on the premises by the artisans you see working. Their work includes bowls, vases, sculptures and a full range of collectibles.

Bailey's Ice Cream Parlour

From here, turn left and walk back up the road. At the junction with Wilkinson Avenue, there is **Bailey's Ice Cream Parlour**, outstanding for its homemade ice cream, which comes in all manner of tempting flavours and colours. Just around the corner from Bailey's, along Wilkinson Avenue, you will come to Bermuda's finest caves.

There are two sets. The first is **Crystal Cave** (April to October: daily 9.30am–4.30pm; November to March: tel: 293 0640 for winter schedule). This one is the larger of the two and was discovered in 1907 by two small boys pursuing a lost ball. Further exploration revealed an underground saltwater lake in the huge cavern. Two of the stalagmites here are said to be over a million years old.

Leamington Cave (March to November: Monday to Saturday 9.30am–4pm) is a little further away; approximately three minutes by bike on Harrington Sound Road, at the end of Wilkinson Avenue. Entrance is with an accompanying guide only and both are worth a visit; Leamington Cave in some respects is more enchanting because it is smaller and its caverns and walkways seem less awesome. It lies within the grounds of the Plantation Restaurant which sometimes offers free entry to the cave to its customers.

Walking or riding between each of the attractions, plus the time taken to enjoy what each has to offer, will provide a very enjoyable and informative morning.

Crystal Cave

3. Devil's Hole and Walsingham

A chance to watch turtles in their natural environment, visit a nature reserve and venture into an area of mangrove swamps.

This is one of Bermuda's oldest tourist attractions, with promotional material dating back to the 1840s. It consists of a small grotto – actually a collapsed cave – which happens to have a small underwater outlet onto the South Shore. This crack through the rocks facilitates a natural and constant inflow of seawater and enables the regular stock of fish to live quite happily without any need for an artificial water circulating system.

Traditionally, **Devil's Hole** – the name is derived from the loud noise sometimes generated by an inward surge of seawater, nothing to do with the 'devils' which the 16th-century shipwrecked sailors believed inhabited these islands – is the home of several turtles, sharks and various local fish (April to October: daily 8am–6pm, November to March: daily 10am–5pm). Because this natural aquarium is circular and rather small, visitors have an excellent opportunity to inspect the sea creatures at uncommonly close quarters, in something approximating their natural environment. Stocks are replenished by the fishermen who live in the neighbourhood. One of the much publicised attractions of Devil's Hole is the chance to lure a turtle, or shark, with bait attached to an unhooked line; with absolutely no danger to the turtles – and hopefully none to yourself – this is a unique chance to get a sense of their sheer weight and watch their eating techniques.

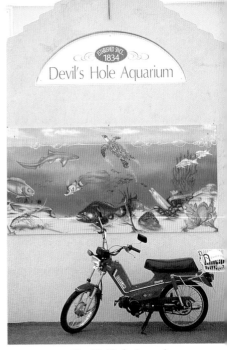

Devil's Hole Aquarium

An incidental anecdote about Devil's Hole: it is said that the 1940s international swimming sensation Esther Williams was visiting this spot when she accidentally dropped her purse in among the sharks and turtles. Quite undaunted she apparently dived in and casually retrieved her valuables. This is not to be recommended to anyone else, however!

It is only a five-minute ride by bus or bike eastwards along Harrington Sound to the exclusive area known as **Walsingham**. The entrance is marked by a sign advertising 'Tom Moore's Tavern', which leads you down Walsingham Lane, a narrow roadway flanked by a hedgerow of Surinam cherries.

Bermuda's principle rock base is limestone, a bedrock which is not only highly porous but which allows rainfall to dissolve pockets of soluble material as it percolates through. The effect of this is that limestone is always pocked by holes, caves and underground caverns. It is in this overall area which we call Walsingham (named after the original house which was built on this vast estate) that Bermuda's major commercial caves are located: Leamington and Crystal (see *Pick & Mix 2*).

Part way down Walsingham Lane, on the left, is the **Idwal Hughes Nature Reserve**. This is a clearly defined portion of land donated by the Hughes family – one of the oldest families on the island – in order to preserve it as a natural habitat for plants and wildlife. A trail leads walkers through dense undergrowth and a fascinating network of collapsed caves and sinkholes. Herons are among the birds most common in this reserve.

A short distance further down this same lane you come to the highly recommended restaurant **Tom Moore's Tavern**, named after the 19th-century Irish poet Tom Moore who briefly held a government post in Bermuda. He spent a short time at the house during his stay on the island and composed a poem about the calabash tree which stands in the grounds. (See the *Excursion to National TrustProperties* for more details about Tom Moore and his amorous reputation.) The house is the one formerly known as Walsing-

Nesting time

ham – the 17th-century seat of the Trott family. By the side of the car-park, on the left, you can step to the edge of a small mangrove swamp and perhaps catch a glimpse of several large specimens of mullet swimming idly among the overhanging vegetation.

At the back of the main house, there is a narrow pathway which weaves through a mixture of hibiscus and cherry bushes. Whilst this, technically, means encroaching temporarily on private land, responsible visitors have rarely been prevented from following this path into **the Jungle**, as it is known locally. First, you pass a superb example of a mangrove swamp; the roots of the trees seem to grow downwards from the upper branches, creating a web of interlacing fingers probing deep into the brackish, detritus-laden waters. From here, the route goes inland for a little while, before finally emerging in a grassy open space with water-bound, collapsed caves at either side. Invariably, fish can be seen swimming in the larger one to the right. There is an abundance of very large succulents of the aloe family, their sharp pointed tips piercing one another in the uncultivated mayhem.

On the far side, the land elevation increases slightly and the vegetation steadily changes into that which Bermudians call upper woodland. There are several fine caves in among the trees and glades, although visitors are dissuaded from attempting to investigate them; the caves do not have properly excavated entranceways, they are not lit in any way nor are they safe for unauthorised, amateur descent. Nevertheless, they are interesting because they are characteristic of the subterranean nature of the Walsingham region of Bermuda.

There are a couple of possible detours along side paths, but eventually the main pathway turns back on itself and you will find yourself back near Tom Moore's Tavern. The best advice is to stick to the main paths and not get lost by being too adventurous.

4. The Serenity of Flatts Village

A morning visit to the Government Zoo and Aquarium, followed by the Railway Museum, with a swim at the end. Bring a picnic for the beach.

Bermuda only has two towns (Hamilton and St George) and just three villages: Somerset, North Village and Flatts. Without doubt Flatts remains one of the most picturesque settings any community could hope to have.

Whether it is approached from St George along the North Shore, or from Hamilton via the Middle Road, the first glimpses are always breathtaking. Flatts is centred upon a narrow inlet which winds inland from the sea and then coils its way beneath a small bridge, into the inland body of water named **Harrington Sound**. Shops are scattered along the sides of the inlet and houses are perched among the adjacent hillsides; a magnificent row of palm

Picturesque Flatts

trees rises from the waterfront and fish swim among the eddies and changing currents of its sparkling waters. In days gone by, Flatts was an anchorage for larger vessels, but today its mooring sites are occupied by pleasure craft. It is believed locally the Flatts was once a smugglers' cove and it is certainly in a good position for it.

Other than a variety of interesting little shops, guest accommodations (Palmetto Bay and Brightside), snack bars noted for home-baked goods, and a couple of condominium developments, the focal point of Flatts is undoubtedly the **Government Zoo and Aquarium** (daily 9am–5pm).

All the fish and sea creatures on display here are natives of Bermudian waters. Occasionally supplemented by finds made by fishermen or casual divers, the bulk of the exhibits – be they sharks, anemones, corals or seahorses – are acquired by the aquarium's own staff, who make regular expeditions out to sea in search of new fish and general display stocks.

Established in the 1920s, the aquarium sits on the eastern side of **Flatts Inlet**, in a position which conveniently allows it access to the waters of Harrington Sound. It operates under the umbrella of a government department, but successfully strives towards being self-supporting, principally through a small entrance fee and the pro-

Parrot fish

ceeds of its shop. Associated with the aquarium is the Zoological Society, which brings members together for a variety of workshops and fundraising projects. The zoo complex also houses a small reference library and facilities for on-site research. You enter through a fine cedar porchway and are soon inside the darkened halls of the main exhibition area. A self-directed tour is available free of charge, incorporating an 'electronic wand' which activates a commentary within designated zones at each tank. For those not interested in such gadgetry, coloured drawings and written descriptions are attached to plaques adjacent to each tank.

As far as possible, displays seek to reconstruct the actual environment in which each species would normally be found. This is a deliberate effort to make the visit into an informative learning experience. Groupings are also in accordance with natural communities, in which each element is dependent upon and compatible with the other. So for example, moray eels glide and squirm among gnarled and pitted rocks; wrasses, urchins and squirrel fish inhabit a rocky ledge near a sandy bottom.

Particularly noteworthy are the tanks which enable you to have a closer look at turtles, lobsters and the elegant angelfish. There are miniature tanks which highlight sealife among the inshore mangrove roots, seahorses, and the nocturnal phosphorescence among corals and smaller life forms.

Stealing a kiss

There is something uncomfortably awesome about the sight of a shark and when it swims past at shoulder height it is even more stunning. It is quite disturbing to have a close-up view of the creature consuming smaller fish – children usually love it. The large, curved tank at the end of the hall is essentially the showpiece of the aquarium, for it seeks to put the visitor directly among those creatures which inhabit the deeper oceanic waters off Bermuda. The tank is designed to simulate the experience of being down among the creatures that live out in the ocean beyond the reefs. Usually, the display includes a range of colourful sealife from schools of snapper through to menacing barracuda and omnipotent sharks.

When you leave this building, you come to two pools: one accommodates a small family of happily frolicking seals; the other takes the form of a lily pond and is home to dozens of bulbous Japanese *koi*. Yet another pool, situated outside by the bus stop, contains more turtles.

At this point, you are free to roam around the small zoo. Here you can see alligators, monitor lizards, raccoons, peacocks, insects (including cockroaches), dozens of parrots and a miscellany of mandarin and mallard ducks. Inconspicuously, somewhere, there is even a solitary barn owl, sitting, watching, and waiting. Lizards inhabit another nearby enclosure; be sure to take time to see the skink – Bermuda's indigenous member of the lizard family.

Alligator in disguise

Particular note should be made of the flamingos and Galapagos tortoises, which have been bred successfully in captivity here, and sometimes exported to populate facilities overseas. This experimental, protectionist and conservational aspect of the staff's work has earned worldwide respect and resulted in Bermuda's participation in all manner of international projects.

Leaving the aquarium, it is only a few minutes walk up along the North Shore, going eastwards, to the **Bermuda Railway Museum** (Tuesday to Saturday 10am–4pm).

Appropriately housed in a former railway station – aptly named Aquarium Station on official maps of the route in the 1930s – this is the only museum in Bermuda devoted solely to that era of transportation history. The Bermuda Railway Company operated a single track system which extended all the way from Somerset to St George. It was a wonderful service, offering passengers one of the most picturesque rides imaginable. Dubbed 'Rattle and Shake', it became part of the landscape of Bermuda. First-class passengers travelled comfortably in wicker chairs while the rest bounced about on hard wooden benches, but the view and the convenience of the service, was there for everyone. Regrettably, it proved to be less successful for its investors than had been expected and interest in it waned when the motor car was finally introduced to Bermuda after World War II. After a short life span of just 17 years, which began optimistically with an exciting ribbon-cutting ceremony in 1931, it was dismantled and sold to British Guiana (now Guyana) in 1948.

To this small museum on the edge of Flatts Village flock thousands of railway devotees. On display are numerous items of memorabilia, including spikes and plates salvaged from the tracks, timetables, signs, notices and advertisements. There is also a small souvenir shop which sells related postcards and a well-illustrated book detailing the short but eventful life of 'Rattle and Shake'.

A total of 33 bridges and trestles had to be erected at various junctures along the route in order to carry the track over inlets and bays. The supports of some of these have survived and a row of them can still be seen clearly marking the route across Flatts Inlet.

From the Railway Museum, a short section of the right-of-way extends all the way up to **Shelly Bay**. This makes for a pleasant and leisurely amble along the shoreline of about 15 minutes' duration and offers the chance for an enticing swim at the end, and a picnic if you brought one (also see *Railway Trails*.)

St Catherine's Fort

5. Exploring the Forts

An afternoon tour of Bermuda's forts, with a swim at Whale Bay.

Bermuda is remarkably well endowed with forts, some of which date from the early 17th century, although most of those on to-day's option are from the 19th century. The majority are entirely accessible to the general public. Most of the others are located on islands situated on the outer edge of St George's Harbour and Castle Harbour and can only be reached from the sea. As Bermuda never suffered a serious attack, most of the forts remain in extremely good condition.

The largest fortification is the Royal Naval Dockyard, in Somerset, but forts both large and small have been erected throughout Bermuda and they make pleasant locations for afternoon picnics and interesting stops. In most cases, they offer excellent views, because their prime function was to serve as early-warning posts or lookouts, to defend the islands from attack.

Other than Dockyard, Fort Hamilton and St David's Battery, each of which is mentioned in greater detail elsewhere, **St Catherine's Fort** (daily 10am–4pm), an excellent example of 19th-century military architecture, is perhaps the next largest. It stands on a promontory on the north-east side of St George's Island and commands a view towards all the entrances through the reefs. Golfers will not fail to be distracted by it as they try to negotiate the complicated 14th green overlooking Coot Pond. This Victorian fortification, with massive stone walls, is built over a warren of tunnels and storage rooms, and includes a large courtyard and impressive gun emplacements. Replicas of the British Crown Jewels are housed in an upper chamber and there are displays of uniforms and guns, as well as a sequence of dioramas depicting Bermuda's early history.

A few minutes further along the northern road, you will come to two other forts. One is **Alexandra Battery**,

Getting around

built in the same period. It was an important command post during World War I, serving as a lookout for passing ships. The small beach to its left is called Buildings Bay and is reputedly the site where the shipwrecked survivors of the *Sea Venture* toiled in 1609 to build the hulls of *Patience* and *Deliverance*, before sailing off towards Jamestown. The site was originally called Frobisher's Buildings Bay, after the ship's carpenter Richard Frobisher who was in charge of the work, but over the years his name was dropped.

A short distance beyond this is **Gates Fort** (daily 10am–4pm), constructed sometime in the 1620s. Today, this small single-roomed fort stands at the entrance to Town Cut – the sole entry into St George's Harbour for cruise ships and other large vessels. Stand here when one is entering and you can virtually touch its portholes.

Gate's Fort

Along the South Shore, in Devonshire, lies Devonshire Bay, an attractive fishing harbour with its own small crescent beach and shallow waters. Situated on the western rim, however, on a promontory and partially concealed amidst woodland, are the remains of the foundations of **Devonshire Bay Battery**. Constructed in the 1860s, its overall configuration has been made more apparent in recent years, thanks to some preliminary archaeological digging.

Two other forts stand on government land up in the West End. **Whale Bay Battery**, completed in 1876, lies in a cliffside park of the same name a short distance beyond Horseshoe Bay. (The park slopes down to a relatively uncrowded beach, if history is making you hot, and you feel like a swim.) The battery commands views out towards a channel through the reef which is still known as Hog Fish Cut and it was claimed that its powerful guns could hit a target 6 miles (9km) out to sea. The remnants of the barracks and ammunition magazine may still be seen, as may the remnants of an earlier, semi-circular fort.

Fort Scaur (daily 10am–4.30pm), built in the 1870s, stands on the highest point of Somerset Island and offers perhaps the best place from which to gaze out over Hamilton Harbour – a view rivalled only by that from Gibb's Hill Lighthouse. It is set slightly back from the road at **Ely's Harbour**, but its presence is clearly marked by signposts. The fort is encircled by low but solid walls, around which are the deep incisions of moat-like trenches. The grounds are carefully maintained and there are a couple of lower chambers to explore but the view is magnificent and Fort Scaur is well worth a visit for this alone. A marker on the northern side of the slope tells you that London is 3,076 miles away.

6. St David's Island

An afternoon trip which takes in St David's Lighthouse, and gives an opportunity to see humpback whales, the NASA tracking station, and some unusual birds in Great Head Park. Bring swimming things for a dip en route and end with a seafood supper at Dennis's Hideaway, tel: 297 0044 or the Black Horse Tavern, tel: 293 9742. It's advisable to book, and bring your own wine if you choose Dennis's Hideaway.

Island tranquillity

If you are travelling by bike, take the road over the Causeway, past the airport and continue up to the roundabout directly in front of the US/NATO base. Instead of taking the road over the bridge to St George, follow that which is clearly marked as St David's Road. Alternatively, take any eastbound bus from Bailey's Bay; ask for a transfer and get off at the Base Gate. From that same stop, take the St David's bus (No 6). (Check your schedule carefully before you start because this is an hourly service.)

The St David's Road winds picturesquely past Emily's Bay, Cocoa Bay and Great Bay, affording delightful views on your left towards distant St George and various islands and inlets. After about six minutes or so, you will pass the St David's Post Office; just beyond here, on the right, is the twisting, curling road which leads straight to St David's Lighthouse. (Check beforehand and see which days the lighthouse is open to the public.)

St David's Lighthouse stands on the eastern tip of Bermuda. It is from here that all ships take their bearings as they gently weave their way through Bermuda's complicated reef pattern; all boats pass near here on their way up the channels leading into the ports of Hamilton and St George. This is also the location of the finishing line for such bluewater, Atlantic yacht races as the Newport–Bermuda and the Marion–Bermuda (held in alternate years). Depending on the wind direction, you may well have flown over it when arriving in Bermuda, because it is directly in the flight path of incoming aircraft.

The view from **Lighthouse Hill** is an uninterrupted panoramic seascape. From here, you can see quite clearly how the reefs follow closely along the South Shore and then gradually start to arc further away from the land, outwards onto the North Shore. This elevation also enables you to see the mosaic of colour variations in the water, where deeps and shallows give way to sandy bottoms. During April and May, humpback

St David's Lighthouse

whales migrate northwards through Bermudian waters and may often be spotted from the vantage point of Lighthouse Hill.

There's something else to see from here, too. If you stand on the water side of the lighthouse and look in the middle foreground along the South Shore, you will notice the satellite dishes of **Cooper's Island**. This facility is the principle NASA Tracking Station for space launches from Cape Kennedy. Since the earliest flights, the primary separation of rockets has always been monitored from Cooper's Island and for many of the first American spacemen this was where they set foot once again on planet Earth. The NASA Tracking Station at Cooper's Island provides conducted tours of its facilities but prior arrangements must be made.

Descend Lighthouse Hill and return to the main road, then turn right and proceed along the waterfront until reaching the little parking lot by a sign for **Great Head Park**. There is a clearly identified pathway leading from the top of the steps all the way around this naturally preserved parkland. It is an interesting walk, lasting about half-an-hour, which takes you among typical wooded hillsides and then back along the top of a sheer cliff. Depending on the season, birdwatchers can expect to see various warblers and finches, but great blue herons and kingfishers can be anticipated year-round. Between March and August, breeding longtails build their nests in the cliff face and their elegant gliding and swooping is a rare sight to behold.

The more adventurous may care to descend (carefully) down the rocks from the early part of the trail and explore the craggy shoreline. Here there are several caves, in which you may see small clusters of Bermuda's delicate maidenhair ferns. Bermuda's ever-popular and abundant 'Sally Lightfoot' crab often sheds her shell along these rocks, a mark not of death, as many suppose, but of another stage of growth. The trail through Great Head Park terminates among the imposing 6-ft (1.80-m) breech-loading guns of the 19th-century **St David's Battery**.

Inviting waters

Dennis in his Hideaway

This military installation, like the majority of the others throughout Bermuda, has seen absolutely no military action whatsoever. Nevertheless, the gun emplacements make for a fascinating place to climb and amble, whilst imagining the noise and chaos which would have resulted had they been called into service. If you are feeling particularly agile and energetic you may care to descend, preferably in rubber-soled shoes, a flight of rock-hewn steps which leads down the precipitous face of Great Head itself; at the base of the cliff, you will see another military lookout post.

From the park and battery area, carry on to the very end of St David's Island. Here you will find a small, quiet beach frequented primarily by St David's Islanders themselves, which is a perfect place to take a dip.

To end the day, have supper on the island. Adjacent to the beach is **Dennis's Hideaway**, noted for its imaginative seafood platters, which include conch fritters and shark hash. The service is very informal and highly personal, with either Dennis or his son Graham on hand to tend to your needs. (I hope you remembered to bring your own wine.) Alternatively, back around the main bay, by the Post Office, is **The Black Horse Tavern**. This is likewise a great place for seafood – the curried conch and fish chowder, in particular, make a splendid prelude to the main course. The water's edge location is a delightful venue from which to watch the setting sun.

7. The Nature Reserves

An afternoon visit to some of Bermuda's most important reserves. Remember to make appointments in advance (except in the case of Spittal Pond).

Heron on lookout

Bermuda is blessed with a number of nature reserves, but you must make an appointment to visit most of them. Contact the Audubon Society, tel: 236 6483, any of the Visitors' Service Bureaux (*see Useful Addresses* in *Practical Information* section) or the National Trust (tel: 236 6483) for details.

Spittal Pond, the island's largest nature reserve, can be visited at any time, without an appointment. Lying to the east of Verdmont, (South Shore Road) its 60 acres (25ha) are home to most of the 25 species of waterfowl which choose to winter in Bermuda. Here, as in other reserves, you are asked to

53

Spittal Pond

keep to the pathways, however tempted you might be to get a closer look at some of the exotic birds. If you visit the reserve during the summer months you may be surprised to see that the waters of Spittal Pond have a distinctive reddish colour. But don't be alarmed: this is simply caused by the mass of red algae which blooms in the pond during summer.

Three other nature reserves lie nearby: **Penhurst Park**, which covers 15 acres (6ha) of the North Shore (Middle Road); the **Arboretum**, also situated on Middle Road, which comprises some 20 acres (8ha) of trees planted mainly for scientific and environmental reasons; and the **HT North Reserve**, also worth a visit, which lies at the western end of Mangrove Lake on the border of Hamilton parish. For bird watching, November to April are the best months to visit the reserves, but even if you are no ornithologist, the parks are fascinating because of the many examples of rare, exotic flowers which thrive on the protected land and in Bermuda's warm climate.

These two reserves make a rewarding half-day trip by themselves and, of course, hours can be spent watching the wildfowl. But if you're in the mood for further investigation, **Paget Marsh**, inland from Hamilton's Harbour Road, is not far away, especially if you are travelling by hired bike or moped.

If you have managed to make an appointment you could spend some time wandering around this 18-acre (7-ha) site, admiring the endangered species of plants and trees which grow there. Or you could save this trip to the marsh for yet another day and combine it with a swim on one of the nearby South Shore beaches.

Cedar forest

1. Visit some National Trust Properties

An excursion which enables you to soak up some of Bermuda's history by exploring some beautifully preserved old buildings.

The Bermuda National Trust is the official custodian of much of the country's architectural heritage and is responsible for preserving and maintaining some of the finest properties in Bermuda. The Trust's very fine headquarters are at **Waterville**, an ancestral home of the Trimingham merchant family, situated near the roundabout in Pompander Gate Road, Paget, on the outskirts of Hamilton (tel: 236 6483). It can be reached within about 20 minutes' walk from the centre of town.

If you are in Bermuda in the spring, enquire at the National Trust office or the Visitors' Service Bureau in Hamilton about the tours which the Trust organises at that time of year of private homes and gardens not usually open to the public, because some of the properties are under private leases, with a conditional clause that they be open to the public at certain times. These include **Palmetto House** (a residence in Devonshire whose wings form the shape of a cross) and **The Old Rectory** (St George), schedules for which can be secured directly from the Trust's headquarters.

Many of the Trust's houses are open to the public in the form of living museums; that is to say, they have been refurbished in keeping with certain historic periods and closely recreate the original atmosphere of the era's bedrooms, kitchens and outbuildings.

Imposing Verdmont

Perhaps the most imposing house of all is **Verdmont**, off Collector's Hill in Smith's Parish. Not only is Verdmont an impressive mansion, built in the style of an English manor house, with many rooms and three different floors to explore, but it also houses the island's best collection of Bermuda cedar furniture including a traditional wooden armchair called a Cromwellian.

In addition to these many fine examples of early furniture, Verdmont also has some superb English china, silverware, Chinese porcelain, prints and portraits. Most delightful is the nursery, strewn with a collection of Victorian toys. The gardens, sloping down to the sea, are a blaze of colour and on the south side give spectacular views of the coast and ocean.

In St George, Trust properties include the Confederate Museum, Tucker House and Bridge House. Even many Americans seem to be unaware of the role played by Bermuda and the Bahamas as commercial centres during the American Civil War, which ended in 1865, but their role was a vital one for ongoing trade. So important was St George in the view of the Confederacy that the government deemed it worthwhile to appoint a permanent commercial agent to the town, one Major Walker. He lived in the building now known as the **Confederate Museum** (Monday to Friday 10am–5pm), on the corner of King's Square, a property which at one time did service as the Globe Hotel. Graced by the portraits of Major Walker and his wife, the museum exhibits all manner of memorabilia dating back to that keystone era of American civil unrest which preceded Lincoln's assassination and the US emancipation of the slaves.

The Old Rectory

The **Tucker House**, on Water Street in St George, was the homestead of the influential Tucker family, descendants of the autocratic Daniel Tucker one of the very earliest governors of Bermuda, a Virginian planter who believed that hanging was the most effective way to deal with miscreants. The family continued to play a very active part in Bermuda's political and commercial life during the 18th century. One distinguished occupant of this house was Henry Tucker, who was the President of the Governor's Council between 1775 and 1800.

The rooms are replete with glass chandeliers and elegant furnishings of English mahogany and Bermuda cedar, the walls are lined with cabinets, various hangings and a fine array of original oil portraits, and the house itself has many interesting architectural features. During the 1860s, one of the back rooms of this house was apparently used as a barber shop by Joseph Hayne Rainey, a freed American slave who escaped to Bermuda at the start of the Civil War and eventually returned to the United States and became the first black man to be elected to the House of Representatives (1870). A small exhibit attests to his brief involvement with the property.

It is said that the Irish poet, Tom Moore, was barred from the Tuckers' properties after he became infatuated with Nea, one of the Tucker wives, and wooed her with indiscreet poems. During his short stay in Bermuda, Moore, who had quite a reputation as

56

a womaniser, appears to have created havoc but in spite of (or because of) this, there is a bust of him in a small, walled garden next to **Bridge House**, just off King's Square.

This house was built to be the residence of a local councillor named Bayley, way back in the 1690s. During the course of its history, it has been home to two governors (the Popple brothers) and also to a noted Virginian privateer named Bridger Goodrich. It is the oldest house in Bermuda which is still used as a domestic residence. It has now been sub-divided into three rented units, of which two are used for everyday living. In the original dining rooms and entranceway, the **Bridge House Art Gallery** exhibits exclusively locally made artwork – in keeping with the tradition established by Bermuda's premier 19th-century silversmiths, the Rankins, who lived and worked in these same rooms over 150 years ago.

At the opposite end of the island, in Sandys Parish, make a point of stopping to visit **Springfield**. This is a wonderful property, with one of the most photographed butteries in the country. A buttery was a small, pointed outbuilding used in the days before refrigeration as a place in which to store food and keep it relatively fresh. Collectively, Springfield's walled gardens, main building, slave quarters and charming rooflines make it a splendid pot pourri of all that is traditional in Bermudian colonial architecture.

In addition to the buildings themselves, Springfield, which was the home of the Gilbert family, sits on the edge of the **Gilbert Nature Reserve**, 5 acres (2ha) of unspoiled land, usually open until dusk.

Also located in glorious grounds is **Camden**, the official residence of Bermuda's premier. Camden is open only on selected days, but a stroll through its 36-acre (15-ha) **Botanical Gardens** is a delight. Camden was built in the 1700s, although its wide, elegant verandahs were added later. Most of the cedar panelling and dining room furniture, was the work of a local craftsman called Jackson. Details of Camden are available from Visitors Service Bureaux.

Camden House

2. Touring the Beaches

Just a few of Bermuda's best beaches, with cliff walks and a visit to Kenny Bascome's famous beach house. Don't forget to take sunscreen.

Bermuda enjoys the well-deserved reputation of having some of the most beautiful beaches to be found anywhere in the world. In part, this is doubtless due to the cleanliness of the sand and the sparkling turquoise waters which continuously douse them. Their famed pink tinge is derived from the fact that small specks of pink coral are generously mixed into the sand itself, which produces a distinctly pinkish complexion.

Perfect bliss

The most popular stretches of sand tend to be along the South Shore where there are no fewer than 23 beaches and coves, because this is the prevailing direction of the ocean currents which move through these waters. Bermuda is affected by the Gulf Stream Drift, a body of warm water which swings through the Caribbean and then curves this way on its journey into the North Atlantic. Its south-westerly origin brings warm water to these islands, which, in turn, helps to promote the growth of a coral reef.

The most extensive lengths of public beach are to be found along the shorelines of Paget, Warwick and Southampton parishes. All are within a 10–20-minute moped ride from Hamilton. The Hamilton/Dockyard No 7 bus also comes this way.

Incidentally, if you come on a spring-time holiday, don't expect to see any locals on the beach, however good the weather, before the last week in May. The story is that Bermudians long ago designated 24 May (Queen Victoria's birthday) as the official beginning of summer and therefore the first day that anyone will swim.

The first beach you'll come to is just below White Sands Hotel, off the Middle Road, in Paget. The public access is directly opposite the entrance to this hotel, at the end of White Sands Road, down an unpaved right-of-way which meanders through an overhanging growth of oleanders and bay grape trees directly onto the beach itself. There are no public facilities and limited shade so it's not ideal for families with young children, or for anybody to spend too much time in the heat of the day, but the location is spectacular and a perfect setting for an early morning swim. Having seen for yourself how lovely it is, you might like to return in the evening for a moonlit dip.

Spectacular South Shore

Cool kids

Bermuda Beach is just round the corner from the Elbow Beach Hotel and opposite the entrance to Horizon's. Approached along a narrow driveway, this particular beach is very popular with Bermudians and, therefore, is a good place to meet the locals. At low tide, beachcombers can enjoy long walks along the sands. At the foot of the steps leading down onto the beach itself stands Dinty's Lunch Wagon, which serves outstanding homemade meat pies and hamburgers, as well as the usual drinks and snacks.

For those who merely want to land on a beach and then walk and walk forever, the best starting point is **Warwick Long Bay**. It is just a short distance further along the South Shore, past the Marley Beach and Longtail Cliffs guest properties. The main road is high above the cliffs at this point, so entry is by a picturesque winding pathway which descends through grass-topped sand-dunes. The dunes have become partially solidified and are dotted with a variety of flowering bushes and the distinctive, spiky Century Plants, members of the lily family, which are also known as American aloes.

From Warwick Long Bay, you can walk with little difficulty all the way to Chapin Bay and on to Horseshoe Bay, Jobsons Cove and so on. In total, the sandy beaches extend along this part of the shore almost without interruption for about a mile. The walk can be made even longer and is particularly delightful if you choose to walk along the

Warwick Long Bay

beaches, paddling in the shallow water, and then return following the well-defined pathways that meander among the sand-dunes.

In the vicinity of **Horseshoe Bay** – which must surely be Bermuda's most photographed beach – there are several cliffs adjacent to the beach and at the water's edge; climbing to the top of their peaks can afford some breath-taking views of the reefs and colour patterns out to sea. Between February and August, hundreds of long-tails make their nests in these cliffs and provide a spectacular sight for birdwatchers.

At Horseshoe Bay a fully-licensed restaurant operates each day, serving meals well into the night. There are also useful facilities such as foot showers and toilets, so this makes a good base, particularly if you are with a group which includes some who like to swim, some who like to walk, a keen ornithologist and someone whose idea of heaven is to sit in the shade with a cold beer and watch other people being energetic.

Diving from these rocks – à la Acapulco daredevils – is dangerous and definitely not to be recommended. And do be very cautious about swimming from any beach, anywhere, on account of the invisible yet omnipresent undertow, which may lure the unwary slowly and steadily into progressively deeper waters.

Continuing westwards into Sandys Parish, there are two charming beaches within easy reach of Somerset Village. The closest is the crescent-shaped **Mangrove Bay**, rimmed with palm trees and right in the centre of the village. A few minutes' ride or walk from Mangrove, is the enticing sweep of **Long Bay**, which looks out over the open sea and is excellent for swimming and snorkelling.

Catching the snorkelling bug

Heading to the east from Hamilton, the most popular public beaches are at **Shelly Bay** and **John Smith's Bay**. The former is a few minutes' ride beyond Flatts Village and the Railway Museum. A favourite beach with locals, it has a large grassed picnic area, as well as a snack bar and changing/toilet facilities. The beach area is shallow in part and wonderful for younger children; but it does get deeper towards the outer edge and is safe for 'floaters' and snorkellers.

John Smith's Bay is on the opposite side of Harrington Sound, on the South Shore, just behind Devil's Hole. This is a carefully landscaped area, which is flanked on either side by rather jagged rocks, and is perfect for those who want to swim, sunbathe, or scramble along the rocky shoreline.

Time to reflect

St George has several major beaches of its own: Tobacco Bay, St Catherine's Beach and Achilles Bay. **Tobacco Bay** is the most popular beach in the East End, where Kenny Bascome and his beach house have become indelible landmarks. The food and local company are good, and there is a well-shaded patio for drinking and relaxing. The beach is very popular because it is well-cared-for, protected, shallow and safe, which makes it a good place for young children, but it also offers plenty of opportunity for stronger swimmers to put on a snorkel and explore the deeper waters around the rocks. Gear can be rented for a nominal fee at the beach house; Kenny will also let you borrow a book when you want a break from swimming or snorkelling. **Achilles Bay** and **Fort St Catherine's Beach** lie either side of the imposing structure of the 19th-century fort at Catherine Point. In the waters off here lies the 1609 wreck of the *Sea Venture* – the ship that carried Sir George Somers and his ill-fated party of Virginia settlers. You are unlikely to come across it by accident, because it lies some distance offshore and, by the time the survivors had finished their salvaging, there was very little left. Nevertheless, it is a remarkable experience to be standing on this beach and know that the survivors from that historic shipwreck actually came ashore at this particular spot.

A few final, friendly words of caution. Always try to avoid exposure to the sun during the hottest part of the day. You may notice that Bermudians themselves are rarely seen on the beaches at mid-day; they swim earlier in the morning, or leave it until the early evening. Because these islands generate virtually no pollution of their own, and are hundreds of miles from everyone else's, the atmosphere here is astoundingly clean and clear. The ultra-violet rays, therefore, are not filtered. The outcome of this is that the Bermudian sun can be quietly vicious and should be treated with considerable care and respect, however much protective sun cream you coat yourself in. Above all else don't lie in the sun too long and never fall asleep.

Blossoms in the sand

Shopping

Bermuda is a delight for any shopper, regardless of whether you are looking for arts and crafts, clothing, jewellery, cameras or liquor packs. Collectors of original watercolours which are uniquely Bermudian should pay a visit to the **Birdsey Studio**, located on Stowe Hill, in Paget (tel: 236 6658). Alfred Birdsey is now officially listed as 'collectible' by one of the leading auction houses in the world. He is a congenial person and a very serious artist who is always willing to discuss his work. Original watercolours start at about $100. Just a few minutes up the road you will come to **Art House** (tel: 236 6746), on the South Road in Paget, by the Paraqueet Restaurant. This is where you will find Joan Forbes – a watercolourist with a relaxed style and appealing subjects.

Local artistry

In Hamilton, I always enjoy going into **The Windjammer Gallery** (tel: 292 7861), on the corner of King and Reid Street – where they have a good selection of originals and prints by local and visiting artists. The Windjammer also have another outlet, showing mainly prints, on Front Street. (The owners represent Desmond Fountain, Bermuda's premier bronze sculptor, so talk to them about arranging to view his work – or contact the **Sculpture Gallery**, tel: 238 8840.) I also like **Heritage House** (tel: 295 2615), which offers an interesting blend of Bermudian and foreign artwork, displayed side-by-side with a selection of antiques and other collectibles. Heritage House is located on Front Street, just past the Bank of Bermuda's multi-storeyed building.

At 18 Queen Street, Hamilton, be sure to visit **Queen Street Glass** (tel: 295 6970), an outlet of the glass blowing factory at Bailey's Bay (*see Pick & Mix 2*), which sells only locally-made glass items of excellent quality. In the same Windsor Place Mall, on the first floor, make time to nip into **State of the Art** (tel: 292 5931) and look at the intricate airbrush artwork of local artist Michael Swan (*see* page 64).

At the extreme ends of Bermuda, there are some excellent places to go hunting for arts and crafts. In Dockyard, call in at the **Bermuda Arts Centre** – a well-arranged gallery exhibiting mainly Bermudian artwork; Chesley Trott, the wood sculptor, also has an open studio here. In an adjacent building is the **Craft Market**, arranged to give the feel of days gone by, where there are always artisans at work. Note, in particular, the cedar doll's-house furniture made by Jack Arnell and his wife.

In the Clocktower Mall, **Michael Swan** has a small studio where he produces much of his fine work; and the Admiral's Locker, a popular place for nautical items, is also in this building. If you're looking for mass-produced prints, go into **Holding's Warehouse**. Whilst at Dockyard, visit the factory of **Island Pottery** where you can both buy ceramics and watch them being made.

In St George, go to Hunter's Wharf, by the main cruise ship terminal, for more craft manufacturing businesses. **Pina** does silkscreen printing on clothes and bags; **Bermuda Beauty Crafts** produces articles in raffiawork. In **The Pottery** next door, the potter is always huddled over a mound of clay. Opposite Dowling's gas station/marina nearby is the **Portcullis**, in which Tony Block produces chess pieces and heraldic plaques and researches family trees.

Up in the town, just off King's Square, is the most diverse selection of arts and crafts in Bermuda: the **Bridge House Art Gallery and Craft Shop**, on Bridge Street, which carries the work of approximately 25 artisans (tel: 297 8211). They were pioneers in this business, they only sell locally-made items and are friendly and helpful. They also have a splendid selection of 'Bermudiana'. Facing the Bridge House entrance, **Bridge Street Men's Shop** has a superb selection of Italian silk ties.

The stores in Hamilton offer merchandise garnered from all over the world. The larger department stores, such as **Triminghams**, **Coopers** (the Wedgwood representative) and **H A & E Smith** (outstanding crystalware), are a delight. **Calypso** sells colourful, fashionable casual wear; **Cecile's** has quality separates and dresses; the **English Sports Shop** is excellent for men's wear; and **Archie Brown's** has a remarkable selection of sweaters and Scottish knitwear. These shops are all very prominent with entrances on Front or Reid streets. If you want something more 'ethnic', go to the northern section of Court Street where you're bound to find something unusual. The best bet for lace and linen is the **Irish Linen Shop** – on Front Street, with another branch tucked away near Mangrove Bay, in Somerset.

For bookworms, Hamilton has the **Book Store** on Queen Street; the **Bookmart**, on the lower floor of the Phoenix Centre on Reid Street; the **Book Rack**, on Burnaby

Cedar craftwork

Nautical knick-knacks

Street; and **Washington Mall Book Store**, in the mall linking Church and Reid streets. In St George, visit the quaint **Book Cellar** on Water Street, located in the cellar of Tucker House. At Dockyard, go to the book shop in the **Clocktower Mall**.

If you are looking for perfume there are locally-made products from the **Bermuda Perfumery**, or 'Royalle Lyme'. Many stores carry their lines. Otherwise, the recognised specialists are **Peniston Brown** and **Guerlain**, with several outlets in Hamilton and St George.

Bermuda is not overrun with antique stores, as most antiques are sold at auctions – dates and locations advertised in newspapers – but the more interesting selections are found at Heritage House (*see* page 63) and at Triminghams (particularly furnishings). Up on Church Street, opposite Hamilton City Hall, is **Timeless Antiques** (tel: 295 5008), which carries a good selection of items, especially old clocks. Behind the city hall, tucked away on Park Road, is **Thistle Antiques** (tel: 292 3839). In St George, seek out **Antiques & Old Stuff**, hidden in the Waterfront Cottage Mall across the road from the Ebenezer Methodist Church on York Street.

Opposite the Princess Hotel, on Pitts Bay Road, is **Pegasus** – my favourite shop for old prints and maps, which occupies the upstairs rooms of a 19th-century house. If your interest lies in china, porcelain, etc, the specialists are **Blucks**, with outlets in Hamilton and St George.

One bargain to which North American visitors gravitate is liquor. Special duty-free packs must be ordered and pre-paid; they are then delivered for collection beyond customs clearance areas at the airport or docks. Check your allowance quotas according to destination. The leading merchants are: **Gosling Brothers**, **Frith's Liquors**, **J E Lightbourne** and **John F Burrows**. **Hand Arnold Ltd** on East Broadway in Hamilton often has bargain prices for over-the-counter buyers; **Bristol Cellars**, on Reid Street, probably have Bermuda's most extensive selection of European wines.

On the Road

There are lots of roadside places where you can grab a quick bite to eat, which is maybe all you need in the heat of the day. Bermudians frequently patronise lunch wagons, which are noted particularly for their homemade pies

Bermuda Beach Wagon

and hamburgers. Their mussel and beef pies are always very popular and tend to sell out quickly. They also serve hot and cold drinks, they are not expensive and they are located everywhere: in car parks and lay-bys and at the beaches. Keep your eyes open – you'll spot them easily.

But if you want a little more variety than a lunch wagon has to offer, and a table to eat at, there are plenty of choices.

Among a host of places where you can eat quickly and casually, the following selection represents good value.

FREEPORT GARDENS
Dockyard
Tel: 234 1692
A full menu of quick meals and good sandwiches.

FROG AND ONION
Opposite the Maritime Museum
Dockyard
Good food in a pub atmosphere.

BRENDA'S POOLSIDE DINER
South Shore Road
Warwick
Tel: 236 7807
Popular selection of snacks and, of course, a pool.

RICHARDSON'S RESTAURANT
North Shore
Pembroke
Tel: 293 9577
More snacks and pizzas.

FAT MAN'S CAFE
Palmetto Road
Devonshire
Tel: 292 0361
Lives up to its reputation for homemade beef pies.

SPECIALITY INN
South Shore
Smith's
Tel: 236 3133

An unusual 'diner' atmosphere, an extensive menu and great pizzas.

THE SWIZZLE INN
Bailey's Bay
Hamilton
Tel: 293 9300
The food is good, although most people stop here for the notorious rum swizzle.

THE LITTLE GREEN FENCE
Flatt's Village
Tel: 293 9288
Good homemade hamburgers.

SHELLY BAY BEACH HOUSE
Shelly Bay
North Shore
Hamilton
Tel: 293 1327
Limited menu, but an ideal spot to eat and swim.

ANGELINE'S
48 York Street
St George
Tel: 297 0959
Homemade pies, cakes and fish sandwiches. Opens for breakfast at about 7am.

The Swizzle Inn

REID'S RESTAURANT
109 Mullet Bay
St George
Tel: 297 1039
Homebaked pies, and a selection of hot and cold snacks.

PINKS
The Walkway, off Front Street
Hamilton
Tel: 295 3524
Homemade desserts, salads and sandwiches and all kinds of delicatessen delicacies.

THE DELI
Washington Mall
Hamilton
Tel: 295 5890
Wonderful pies and hot sausage rolls at very reasonable prices.

DOROTHY'S COFFEE SHOP
Reid Street
Hamilton
Tel: 292 4130
Excellent sandwiches and cakes in a friendly atmosphere.

THE FLYING CHEF AND BEER GARDEN
Off Washington Lane
Hamilton
Tel: 295 1595
Eat in a courtyard amid palms, to the sound of Tyrolean music: Serves fish and chips and schnitzels.

Sno-kones for sale

ROBERTSON'S RESTAURANT
Water Street
St George
Good range of sandwiches and fast foods.

Dining Out

There are many outstanding places to eat in Bermuda, each offering its own ambiance and cuisine. Bermudians tend to dress rather smartly when they are going out in the evenings, so even places which state 'casual dress' may be a little more formal than most visitors would expect.

The following is a selection of good-quality restaurants, to suit just about every taste.

CHOPSTICKS
City Inn Building
Hamilton
Tel: 292 0791
Interesting Thai food.

THE NEW QUEEN RESTAURANT
Par-le-Ville Road
Hamilton
Tel: 295 4004/292 3282
Chinese.

BOMBAY CYCLE CLUB
75 Reid Street
Hamilton
Tel: 292 0048
Indian.

ROSA'S CANTINA
Reid Street
Hamilton
Tel: 295 1912
Mexican.

LA TRATTORIA
Washington Lane
Hamilton
Tel: 292 7059
Italian.

Dining al fresco

TOM MOORE'S TAVERN
Walsingham Lane, off Harrington Sound Road, Hamilton
Tel: 293 8020
Seventeenth-century dining room. Impeccable service, high-quality food and prices to match.

THE BLACK HORSE TAVERN
St David's
Tel: 293 9742
Excellent seafood, including chowders and mussel stews.

DENNIS'S HIDEAWAY
25 Battery Road
St David's
Tel: 297 0044
More good seafood, conch fritters and shark hash are specialities. Take your own wine and relax.

FOURWAYS
Middle Road
Paget
Tel: 236 6517
Elegant atmosphere, excellent food; renowned for desserts. Expensive.

ONCE UPON A TABLE
Serpentine Road
Hamilton
Tel: 295 8585
Gourmet food, great presentation, attractive decor.

CARRIAGE HOUSE RESTAURANT
Water Street
St George
Tel: 297 1270
Good Sunday brunches, as well as outstanding evening meals.

MARGARET ROSE
St George's Club
Rose Hill, St George
Tel: 297 1301
The food and decor almost match the view over the harbour.

MR ONIONS
Atlantic House, Par-le-Ville Road
Hamilton
Tel: 292 5012
Good food in 1920s atmosphere. Full bar and special 'early bird' prices.

WHARF TAVERN
St George
Tel: 297 1515
Informal pub atmosphere. Good food at reasonable prices.

TIO PEPE
South Shore Road
Southampton
Tel: 238 1897
Mainly Italian food.

FLANAGAN'S IRISH PUB
Front Street
Hamilton
Tel: 295 8299
Relaxed atmosphere, cheerful service.

WATERLOT INN
Southampton
Tel: 238 0510
Bayside location, elegant decor.

All the major hotels have outstanding dining rooms in which world-class chefs prepare international dishes.

HAMILTON PRINCESS
Pembroke
Tel: 295 3000

SOUTHAMPTON PRINCESS
Southampton
Tel: 238 8000

ELBOW BEACH HOTEL
Paget
Tel: 236 3535

MARRIOTT'S CASTLE HARBOUR
Tucker's Town
Tel: 293 2040

NEWSTEAD
Harbour Road
Tel: 236 6060
Delightful harbour views.

WATERLOO HOUSE
Pitt's Bay Road
Pembroke
Tel: 295 4480
More romantic harbour views for moonlit evenings.

Bermudians also enjoy brunch – that curious and luxurious meal hovering somewhere between breakfast and lunch. Four places excel in this category – all are mentioned above, with addresses and telephone numbers: Carriage House – always good value; Waterlot Inn – complete with traditional jazz; Elbow Beach Hotel – gourmet food in elegant surroundings and Marriott Castle Harbour, where the staff may call it breakfast, but the local diners regard it as brunch. Try the Marriott's coffee and excellent omelettes.

Take your pick

Nightlife

Bermuda has many nightclubs, each offering its own brand of entertainment. In addition to shows featuring international and local acts, special performances by Bermudian and visiting celebrities may be scheduled at short notice. Newspapers and hotel reception desks carry details of what is offered.

For a special treat, try to locate where the **Gombeys** are performing. This is Bermuda's premier native dance-form and although the purest troupes are street-performers, there have been several successful efforts to corral some of the best Gombey dancers into the nightclub setting.

In Hamilton, and island-wide, a variety of bars and restaurants provide limited, but live, local entertainment at night, and the nightclubs at the larger resort hotels also have shows. In particular, check out the two **Princess Hotels**, **Elbow Beach** and **Sonesta** for cabaret and revue-type shows. Their nightly schedules are always clearly advertised and are patronised by Bermudians.

For those seeking less formal surroundings the following invariably offer live entertainment and are worth a visit. Be prepared to stay up until the early hours because most nightspots become busier and a lot more fun the later it gets.

HENRY VIII RESTAURANT
South Shore
Southampton
Tel: 238 1977

HOG PENNY
Burnaby Hill
Hamilton
Tel: 292 2534

WHARF TAVERN
Water Street
St George
Tel: 297 1838

SHOW BIZ
Corner of King and Reid Street
Hamilton
Tel: 292 0676
A wonderful old Wurlitzer plays golden oldies

THE CLUB
Bermudiana Road
Hamilton
Tel: 295 6693
Above the Little Venice Restaurant, popular with young people. A pleasing environment in which to chat, dance or listen to the latest sounds.

CLUB 21
Dockyard
Tel: 234 2721
Features local jazz musicians.

Sunset sailors

SPARROW'S NEST
Reid Street
Hamilton
Tel: 295 3013
Another jazz venue.

HUBIE'S BAR
Angle Street
Hamilton
Tel: 293 9287
For a soulful night of jazz and blues.

THE SWINGING DOORS
Court Street
Hamilton
Tel: 293 9267
High-powered evenings for those willing to let their hair down.

THE SPINNING WHEEL
Court Street
Hamilton
Tel: 292 7799
More raw sights, sounds and talents.

THE CLAYHOUSE INN
North Shore
Pembroke
Tel: 292 3193
Regularly stages a 'Native Revue', with limbo dancers, etc.

Night cruising

Several boat operators organise night-time trips; some serve drinks only, others have full menus and some offer on-board entertainment. Contact *Lady Tarmara* (tel: 236 0127) or Reef Roamers (tel: 292 8652), Sundeck Too (tel: 293 2640) and *MV Bermuda Longtail* (tel: 292 0282) for details.

Cinemas

Bermuda has two cinemas in Hamilton: the Little Theatre, which offers an optional movie/meal combination with the nearby Chancery Lane Wine Bar, and the Liberty Theatre; and one in Dockyard, the Neptune. Check local papers for programmes.

Live Theatre

Bermuda is rich in amateur performers and very active theatrical societies, but you will need to check with hotel receptions or a current newspaper to see what may be on during your visit. Several local drama companies use the theatre in the City Hall, Hamilton, for productions of plays by local and more celebrated international playwrights.

There is also the **Daylesford Theatre** on Dundonald Street, Hamilton (tel: 292 0848) – the home of the Bermuda Musical & Dramatic Society. The **Gilbert and Sullivan Society** and **Bermuda Philharmonic** also arrange regular programmes, as does the highly acclaimed **Jackson School of Dance** (tel: 292 5815).

The **Bermuda Festival** during January and February is a cultural feast of the visual arts. Contact: Bermuda Festival Office, 8 Front Street, Hamilton (tel: 295 1291).

$\mathbf{A}$s the following list shows, most of Bermuda's festivals are celebrated in the open air, and many of them involve sporting events.

JANUARY / FEBRUARY

Bermuda Marathon/Half Marathon international races.

Bermuda Festival (International Arts Festival) which embraces just about everything from organ music to modern jazz, from barbershop quartets to plays and aerobatic displays – contact Bermuda Festival Office, tel: 295 1291 for details.

Annual Regional Bridge Tournament.

Lobster Pot Golf Tournament held at Castle Harbour.

Bermuda Golf Festival (into March also).

Valentine's Mixed Foursome at St George Golf Course.

MARCH / APRIL

Bermuda Round Dance Festival.

Bermuda Square Dance Convention.

Bermuda All-Breed Championship Dog Show.

Annual Street Festival (entertainment, crafts etc.).

Bermuda College Weeks (for visiting students).

Pro-Am Easter Lily Golf Tournament (for women players).

Easter Rugby Classic (international competition).

Bermuda Youth Football Cup (local and foreign teams).

Open Houses and Gardens (properties open to public).

Agricultural Show (the closest we have to a County Fair).

Peppercorn Ceremony (pomp and pageantry focusing on the State House in St George).

MAY / JUNE

Heritage Month – continuous events and displays.

Beating of the Retreat Ceremonies (military and pipe bands in impressive nighttime displays, held every week alternately in Hamilton, Dockyard and St George in summer).

Queen's Birthday parade

International Yacht Race Week.
Daytona-Bermuda Yacht Race.
Bermuda Day Parade (24 May).
The End-to-End Walk (Charity walk).
Fitted Dinghy Races (24 May).
Queen's Birthday Parade (21 June).
Single-handed Newport-Bermuda Yacht Race (odd years).
Newport-Bermuda Yacht Race (even years).
Marion-Bermuda Yacht Race (alternate years).
Annapolis-Bermuda Ocean Yacht Race (even years).

JULY / AUGUST

Cup Match (two-day cricket festival of East vs. West).
Round-the-Island Powerboat Race.
Bermuda Hockey Festival (sometimes into September).

SEPTEMBER / OCTOBER

Bermuda Triathlon.
International Yacht Races in Great Sound.
Omega International Gold Cup Yacht Races.

NOVEMBER / DECEMBER

Opening of Parliament (a state occasion with a traditional ceremony and parade with all the trimmings).
Bermuda All-Breed Dog Show.
Remembrance Day (for those killed in action).
World Rugby Classic (international team competition).

Round-the-Island race

Bermuda Lawn Tennis Competition.
Bermuda Goodwill Golf Tournament.
Christmas celebrations and parades throughout the island.
Boxing Day – a time of good will and rare appearances by the dancing Gombeys.

Traditional Gombey dance

GETTING THERE

By Air

There are regular daily flights from most major cities on the US eastern seaboard. New York is only about an hour's flying time away. Canadians have access to Bermuda through either Toronto or Halifax, although numerous other connections can be made through any US gateway city. Flying time from Toronto is a little over three hours.

Airlines regularly serving North America include Air Canada, Continental, NorthWest, Delta, US Air, United Airlines and American Airlines. These carriers usually have timed connections with the West Coast, the Caribbean, Central and South America and Asia.

Visitors from Europe may fly direct via British Airways, which has regular flights from the London terminal at Gatwick. Departures are dovetailed to link up with arrivals and departures from other European centres, with minimal inconvenience and delays.

Alternatively, visitors from Europe may fly to any major North American city then join one of the regular connecting flights into Bermuda.

By Sea

Cruise ships operate on a scheduled basis, usually between April and October when the North Atlantic is less turbulent.

Weekly sailings depart from a variety of East Coast ports. Most originate from the New York area, but some come from Florida and the Carolinas. The shorter trips take seven days in all, with three days in Bermuda. The ocean passage takes about 36 hours.

Cruising into port

Other vessels making longer cruises to the Caribbean pay intermittent visits, stopping here for a short while on their way south, or calling briefly on their way back.

Bermuda is also on the regular path for yachts of all shapes and sizes, travelling to and from the West Indies, and from Europe and the Mediterranean to North America. Approval to keep a yacht in Bermuda over the winter must be obtained from local immigration authorities. Vessels staying longer than six consecutive months are eligible for import duty.

A small-sized yacht can expect to reach Bermuda from the US mainland in anything from five to eight days. Racing yachts participating in the classic Newport-Bermuda Ocean Race (held bi-annually) usually make the passage in three days or so. A 35-ft (10.67-m) yacht heading towards the Bahamas would normally allow eight to 10 days; to the Azores, the same skippers would allow two to three weeks.

TRAVEL ESSENTIALS

When to Visit

Bermuda can be enjoyed at any time of the year. The weather is hotter and more humid between May and October, which is the best time of year for those who are primarily interested in swimming and sunbathing.

Golfers and tennis players may prefer cooler conditions, while visiting historical sites and other places of interest is an all-year activity. Many visitors from the Eastern parts of Canada and the United States find Bermuda an ideal refuge from the snow, chills and winter blues of the North American winter.

Summer temperatures are consistently in the upper 80s and low 90s Fahrenheit (30°–34°C); humidity is invariably in the 90s (32°–36°C). Between November and March temperatures average somewhere in the low 60s (17°C), but the humidity may well be in the 40s (5°–8°C) making it comfortably cool. There is no special rainy season; the annual total is slightly less than 60ins (152cm).

Passports and Visas

All visitors to Bermuda are required to posess proof of citizenship, a current passport or official photo-identity. Non-residents entering the country must have a return ticket in order to be granted landing permission.

Visas are not normally required from British Commonwealth citizens, nor from those normally resident in North America. By virtue of a special reciprocal provision, Americans may not be obliged to bear a passport.

Not all European nations have mutual non-visa arrangements with the Bermuda government and visitors are advised to check with their local authorities. The same applies to residents of Central America, South America, parts of Africa and Asia. Visitors from these areas who intend reaching Bermuda via Canada or the United States should verify that they have the correct documentation. Countries whose citizens do require visas include China, Morocco, Jordan, Mongolia, Bosnia and Hungary.

No innoculations or health certificates are mandatory, under normal circumstances. However, travellers from countries which have experienced recent or prolonged outbreaks of contagious, communicable diseases are advised to check their status with the relevant medical authorities prior to departure.

Customs

No item which has been made from an animal on any international protected species list may be brought into these islands. This would include anything made from ivory, alligator shoes, snake belts and suchlike. The importation of livestock is not permitted unless prior clearance has been granted.

These islands are also traditionally intolerant of any efforts to import illegal drugs. Convicted traffickers in narcotics, regardless of quantities and whether for personal use or otherwise, are heavily fined and liable to imprisonment or instant deportation. Under the Misuse of Drugs Act, convictions carry a fine of up to $10,000 and/or 5 years' imprisonment. The possession of firearms is also illegal.

Departing guests are permitted to take unlimited gifts and other purchases out of Bermuda, regardless of monetary value. Some restrictions are imposed on the export of locally-made antiques and similar items of 'Bermudiana' of recognisable historical value, which may require prior documented approval. The harvesting of living corals, shells, etc is strictly prohibited in Bermuda.

Visitors returning to, or travelling through the United States, are processed by US Customs and Immigration Officials prior to departure from Bermuda.

Dressed for business

What to Wear

Bermuda does not have four distinct seasons. A hot, humid summer period, which lasts for virtually half the year, is followed by an unpredictable phase, between November and March, characterised by lower humidity, winds and intermittent rainfall (*see When to visit* for average temperatures).

Pack a sweater and light raincoat and a jacket or coat for the evenings during the cool season. Between June and September locals wear light casual clothes and men go off to the office in smart jackets and their famous Bermuda shorts. Worn with a conventional jacket, shirt and tie, these are considered suitable for almost any occasion.

Bird's eye view

Strict laws prohibit men from going bare-chested, and ban women from wearing costumes which might be construed as too revealing. On the whole, clothing styles are somewhat conservative. 'Smart casual' is the usual password for nightclubs and restaurants – although there is a tendency for Bermudians to dress very smartly or formally, regardless.

Weights, Distances and Electricity

Bermuda uses the Imperial system, but some goods and measurements are in metric form.

Electricity outlets normally operate on 110/120 volts, but some electrical sockets are calibrated at 220 volts. Always double check. Because power is generated from imported petroleum oil the cost of electricity here is astronomical.

Time Differencies

Bermuda follows the international practice of adopting Summer Time and Winter Time. Therefore, it is usually one hour ahead of New York, two hours ahead of Toronto and four hours ahead of Vancouver and San Francisco, four hours behind London time, five hours behind Germany and six hours behind Moscow.

GETTING ACQUAINTED

Geography

Bermuda is a cluster of islands, surrounded by a coral reef. It is 650 miles (1,046km) off the coast of North America and a little over 3,500 miles (5,700km) from northern Europe. The islands were formed around the rim of a long-extinct volcano which erupted from the ocean bed. The islands cover a total area of approximately 22sq miles (57sq km).

The landscape is gently undulating, the shoreline marked by bays and inlets. Most of the beaches are along the south shore, where their pinky coloured sand, washed by very clear water, affords spectacular scenery. The encircling reef can be seen quite plainly from these beaches. The reef is reputedly the most northerly living coral reef in the world.

The dominant rocks are limestone and sandstone, the latter formed from ancient fossilised dunes. There are some outstanding inland caves – particularly in the Walsingham region at Bailey's Bay, where Crystal and Leamington caves are open to the public.

There is virtually no surface freshwater, other than brackish ponds and marshes scattered throughout all parishes. There are no rivers at all. Drinking water is obtained by collecting rainwater on rooftops and storing it in special tanks. There are some desalination plants, but conversion costs are high.

Population

According to the latest government statistics, Bermuda has a population of 58,460. Of these, 33,808 are black and 21,159 are white. Universal suffrage, granting voting rights to all adults, became law in 1963.

Religion

According to the 1991 census, the denomination with the largest congregation in Bermuda is the Anglican Church, the religion brought by the original settlers. The next largest groups are Catholics and members of the AME Church (African Methodist Episcopal) but there are 17 different religious affiliations, the smallest communities being Ethiopian Orthodox, Jewish and Baha'is.

Government and Politics

Bermuda is a self-governing British colony. Britain's sole areas of responsibility cover internal security and external defence. Although a governor is appointed to represent the Crown, the country rules itself and elects its own officials.

It is a constitutional democracy, operating through a two-tiered Parliament: a Lower House of 40 elected members and an Upper House, or Senate, to which members are appointed. The leader of the majority party becomes the premier of Bermuda. There are three political parties: United Bermuda Party (UBP); the Progressive Labour Party (PLP) and the National Liberal Party (NLP).

Since 1968, Bermuda has followed its own constitution, in which the rights of individuals regardless of race, creed or religion are fully protected. A Human Rights Commission oversees the preservation of those provisions. There is also a Race Relations Council.

Smiles for the camera

Education

The Bermuda government operates a system which guarantees free education for all children. Fully-equipped schools are maintained at the nursery, primary and secondary levels. Students wishing to continue on to further education at the Bermuda College pay minimal course fees, which are subsidised by the governing body, through the government.

The educational system itself is modelled on the British one and tends to follow British practice in most respects, although most of the curricula are locally evolved and orientated. The majority of external examinations are identical to those taken by children and young people in the United Kingdom.

MONEY MATTERS

Currency

Bermuda has its own money, which is carefully floated alongside the value of the US dollar. Coins include: 5¢, 10¢, 25¢, 50¢ and $1. Paper money is also in circulation, with notes for: $2, $5, $10, $20, $50 and $100.

Shop keepers will usually accept American currency, as a convenience and service to travellers, but they are not obliged to do so. The rate across the counter is dollar-for-dollar. All other currencies must be changed at local banks, where the official daily rates of exchange are posted.

All the major credit cards may be used in Bermuda, with sums over $150 invariably subjected to an on-the-spot transaction authorisation through the issuing company. Visa and Mastercard are the most commonly used cards, followed by American Express; selected outlets may also accept Diners and Discovery cards. All travellers cheques issued through internationally recognised agencies are acceptable in Bermuda. It is recommended, for ease of transactions, that travellers cheques be bought in US dollars.

Service with a smile

Tipping

The majority of restaurants and hotels include an automatic gratuity, which is added on to all bills. The percentage varies from place to place, but will be publicly indicated somewhere on the premises. Visitors staying at hotels and guest houses are advised to clarify the nature and extent of service gratuities and any other taxes which are liable to be added to final bills. As with most other places, it is usual to tip taxi drivers about 10 percent of the fare.

There is a government Occupancy Tax of 6 percent in all hotels. This information is readily available upon request, or can be ascertained in writing prior to making a reservation. Such 'extras' can only be instituted after Bermuda government approval – all aspects of tourism are carefully monitored by the government, including product quality, hygiene and service, and comments are eagerly solicited from all visitors.

Taxes

Bermuda is an unusual country, in that its citizens pay neither income tax, nor purchase tax; there are no federal taxes added to invoices, nor state taxes, nor VAT. If this sounds Utopian, then it does indeed come close to it.

There is an annual land tax – based upon the government's assessment of each property's annual rentable value (ARV). Much of the revenue comes from Customs duties, because almost everything is imported into this non-industrialised country; duty is charged on the importer at point of entry. This adds to the cost of the item, as does freight and insurance – hence Bermuda's high prices.

The significance of this to visitors, is that you pay precisely whatever price is marked on all merchandise. There are no added extras to pay. The exception to this are the hotel occupancy tax, mentioned above, and an airport departure tax of $15. This is not a tourist tax: Bermudians also have to pay it. Cruiseship passengers pay $60, but this is pre-paid in their vacation package.

GETTING AROUND

In a commendable effort to control traffic congestion, the government restricts cars to one vehicle per household. None are available for rent to residents or visitors. The speed limit is 20 mph (35 kmph) and we drive on the *left*. Travelling about these islands, nevertheless, is easy and there are many different options.

Buses

A comprehensive bus service enables passengers to travel from one end of Bermuda to the other with ease. The buses are very comfortable European imports and their schedules are available free from hotel reception desks, the Hamilton Bus Terminal (tel: 295 4311) and all Visitors Service Bureaux. They include timetables and a colour-coded map identifying the individual routes.

Blocks of tickets and special passes are available through all post offices, as well as the central terminal in Hamilton. If you pay when boarding a bus you must have the correct change. Tickets are valued for either three or 14 zones, depending on distance. Passengers wishing to break their journey should request a transfer ticket, immediately upon boarding the bus. This permits a sightseeing stop-off and is valid for an hour or so.

Rented Mopeds

Mopeds can be rented from dozens outlets. Anyone above the age of 16 is permitted to drive a motorized cycle on public roadways and this offers flexibility and individual freedom. There are many cycle liveries and most offer a collection and delivery service. Several of the larger hotels – such as Elbow Beach and Marriot's Castle Harbour – operate rentals.

Rates vary according to type of vehicle and operate on a daily or weekly basis. Third party insurance and a deposit are always required and crash helmets must be worn. All hiring establishments must explain how to operate the vehicle, and the larger ones also offer

Romantic road names

an opportunity to practise before going on the road. Many have small test grounds adjacent to their premises and booklets which explain the Highway Code.

This is a pleasurable way to see Bermuda, but there is obviously an element of danger when travelling unknown roads. Remember that Bermudians drive on the *left* as in Britain; most accidents occur when drivers keep looking behind; roads are frequently narrow and winding, with countless 'blind spots'; the official speed limit is only 20 mph (35 kmph) but accidents happen. One final note, Bermudians have a cheery habit of hooting when they pass friends on the roads. Don't misinterpret this as irritation with slow-moving and wobbling tourists.

Ferries

Coordinated to mesh with bus times and offering inter-usable tickets, ferries are an enjoyable way to see Bermuda. They are a conventional commuter service for Bermudians, being convenient and relatively inexpensive (Hamilton Ferry Terminal, Albouy's Point, tel: 295 4706). They operate only within the Great Sound, linking Hamilton and Bermuda's western extremities with the Paget, Warwick, Southampton and Sandys shoreline. The routes meander among the islands and afford some lovely scenery. Bikes can be taken on board all ferries.

Easy rider

Bicycles

Conventional pedal cycles can also be rented. A list of hirers can be found in various local publications, and in the Yellow Pages. The same traffic warnings apply. Also be aware of the dangers of dehydration, particularly during hotter months. Although locals jog and cycle at all times of day, don't forget that they are used to these conditions.

Horse and Carriage

By day or night, this is a delightful way to see Bermuda. All prices are government controlled. A few carriages operate daily outside of Hamilton, where the official carriage terminal is on Front Street.

Taxis

Bermuda's taxi drivers displaying a blue flag on the bonnet are government-qualified guides and are a font of local knowledge; ask about their special tour rates and routes. Rates are fixed by the government and recorded on internal meters; this is easy for a receipt. Most carry portable machines for credit cards. All rates increase after 10pm.

Bermuda Day:	24 May
Queen's Birthday:	21 June
Cup Match/	
Somers Day:	last weekend of July
Labour Day:	1 September
Remembrance Day:	11 November
Christmas Day:	25 December
Boxing Day:	26 December

Where public holidays fall on a Saturday or Sunday, they are usually observed on the following Monday.

ACCOMMODATION

Because of the importance of tourism to Bermuda's reputation and economy, the government carefully regulates and monitors all local accommodation.

Any travel agent can supply a comprehensive list of hotels, or you can write directly to the Bermuda Department of Tourism at Global House, PO Box HM 465, Hamilton. Each hotel offers its own ambiance, personality and services. When selecting accommodation, therefore, you should consider its location – sea views, beach accessibility, sporting facilities and proximity to places of interest. It's not always easy to recommend one place over another, but those I have listed have always appealed to me personally and have that extra something which sets them apart from the rest.

Price rates vary according to time of year, so ask for listings and special package deals. Rates are posted inside each room. Various food plans are available and several hotels offer inter-changeable dining arrangements. The rates here are per person, sharing a double room. The dollar ratings reflect the comparative overall cost of staying at each place, and the accommodation is grouped into categories as follows:

$$$$=$100 –$295
$$$=$100 –$180
$$=$70 –$135
$=$40 –$85

Resort Hotels

(All the hotels listed in this section offer complete luxury services and full on-site facilities, which are specified below each individual entry.)

HOURS AND HOLIDAYS

Business Hours

Most stores are open Monday to Saturday 9am–5.30pm. Almost nothing is open on Sunday. Banks open Monday to Thursday 9.30am–3pm; some open a little later on Friday and all close on Saturday.

Public Holidays

New Year's Day:	1 January
Good Friday:	variable

SONESTA BEACH
South Shore Road
Southampton Parish
Tel: 809-238 8122; Fax: 809-238 8463
403 suites; private waterfront/beaches; freshwater pools; all-day meal service; shops; salon; golf; tennis courts; diving instruction; night club. **$$$$**

SOUTHAMPTON PRINCESS
South Shore Road
Southampton Parish
Tel: 809-238 8000; Fax: 809-238 8968
600 suites; among the most luxurious in the world; tennis courts; private beach with restaurant; golf; overlooks Hamilton Harbour and South Shore; restaurants and nightclubs on property. **$$$$**

HAMILTON PRINCESS
Pitts Bay Road
Hamilton
Tel: 809-295 3000; Fax: 809-295 1914
456 suites; within walking distance of central Hamilton; free transportation to beach; overlooking harbour; first class restaurants, shops, bars, nightclub on premises. **$$$$**

MARRIOTT'S CASTLE HARBOUR
Tuckers Town
Smith's Parish
Tel: 809-293 2040; Fax: 809-293 8288
415 suites; 20 minutes from Hamilton and St George; set in landscaped grounds with first-class golf course; swimming pool and beaches; lounge; nightclub; restaurants include Mikado – outstanding for Asian food. **$$$$**

ELBOW BEACH HOTEL
South Shore
Paget Parish
Tel: 809-236 3535; Fax: 809-236 8043
298 suites; on a hillside overlooking South Shore; own waterfront and beach; full services including cycle livery; dining rooms, shops and nightclub on premises; variety of room/meal plans. **$$$$**

BELMONT HOTEL
Middle Road
Warwick
Tel: 809-236 1301; Fax: 809-236 6867
154 suites/rooms; adjacent to golf course; splendid views over Hamilton Harbour and countryside; full restaurant and night club facilities; shops on premises; relaxing country club atmosphere. **$$$$**

Smaller Hotels
(Offering excellent services, first class accommodation and the majority of facilities either in the grounds or close by.)

THE REEFS
South Shore Road
Southampton Parish
Tel: 809-238 0222: Fax: 809-238 8372
65 units; on cliffside overlooking reefs and Christian Bay; pool, dining room – excellent for lunchtime sandwiches – nightly entertainment; tennis courts, swimming and nearby golf courses. **$$$$**

WATERLOO HOUSE
Pitts Bay Road
Hamilton
Tel: 809-295 4480; Fax: 809-295 2585
34 units; picturesque location on harbourfront with easy access to all facilities in Hamilton; attractive courtyard setting; gourmet food. **$$$**

PALMETTO BAY
Flatts
Smith's Parish
Tel: 809-292 2323; Fax: 809-293 8761
42 units; mid-way between Hamilton and St George; good bus service; own pool and beach; English-style pub; limited nightly entertainment; excellent arrangements for water sports from own dock. **$$**

individual apartments, with two or three similar units forming one·single cottage, frequently situated in a secluded setting surrounded by manicured gardens. Most cottage colonies have swimming pools and many of those along the South Shore have private beaches.

HARMONY CLUB
South Shore Road
Paget
Tel: 809-236 3500; Fax: 809-236 2624
71 units; caters for couples only; price includes everything from food to moped rental; lounge; gardens; pool; bar; tennis courts and nightly entertainment. $$$

NEWSTEAD
Harbour Road
Paget
Tel: 809-236 6060; Fax: 809-236 7454
49 rooms; in quiet residential area of Paget parish; superb harbour and sunset views; private dock, pool and saunas; a delightful old homestead with a charming atmosphere. $$$

ROSEDON
Pitts Bay Road
Hamilton
Tel: 809-295 1640; Fax: 809-295 5567
43 units; residential outskirts of Hamilton; charming 19th-century home; lounges, gardens, breakfast service and pool; free transport to Elbow Beach and exceptionally helpful staff. $$

MERMAID BEACH CLUB
South Shore Road
Warwick
Tel: 809-236 5031; Fax: 809-326 8784
73 units; outstanding South Shore views and secluded beach; pool; limited facilities, but easy access to all parts of Bermuda – Hamilton 15 minutes away by bus. $$

Cottage Colonies
Cottage Colonies offer the perfect solution for those who seek the luxury and attention of larger hotels, yet prefer more intimate surroundings. Accommodation is in

ARIEL SANDS
South Shore
Devonshire Parish
Tel: 809-236 1010
On South Shore, a 10-minute bus ride from Hamilton; private beach, tennis courts, pool; attractive dining room and lounge area; some local entertainment; relaxed atmosphere. $$

PINK BEACH CLUB
South Shore Road
Smith's Parish
Tel: 809-293 1666
81 units; idyllic setting on South Shore with private beaches; freshwater pool; tennis courts; nightly entertainment; close to golf courses; first class cuisine. $$$

LANTANA COLONY CLUB
Ely's Harbour
Somerset
Tel: 809-234 0141; Fax: 809-234 2562
65 units scattered around a 20-acre (8-ha) estate, located amidst secluded gardens; private pool, beach, dock and solarium; good cuisine and varied menu; tennis courts, a putting green and a croquet lawn. $$$

FOURWAYS INN
Middle Road
Paget
Tel: 809-236 6517; Fax: 809-236 5528
10 suites; quiet setting in residential area; easy bus and ferry access to Hamilton; private pool, set in well-tended gardens; outstanding gourmet food; bar; full room service available. $$$

Guest Houses
These properties offer a very informal holiday in which you will enjoy individual attention and get to know the staff and owners as well as enjoying their homes and gardens.

GREENE'S GUEST HOUSE

Middle Road
Southampton
Tel: 809-238 0834; Fax: 809-238 8980
6 units; unpretentious, congenial modern home; hilltop views overlooking the Great Sound; nice rooms with VCRs, air-conditioning, etc; pool, terrace, lounge and dining room. A family business, in which everyone seems to enjoy having guests. $

LOUGHLANDS

79 South Road
Paget
Tel: 809-236 1253
25 units; a distinguished building with well-manicured gardens; pool, tennis courts and patio; dining-room, and an inviting lounge with high Victorian ceiling; close to beaches and Hamilton. $

HILLCREST GUEST HOUSE

Nea's Alley
St George
Tel: 809-297 1630
11 units; this is the place for the personal touch; in its own gardens in the picturesque back streets of St George, with easy access to shops, beaches and bus services. $

Housekeeping Cottages and Apartments

This type of accommodation represents an ideal way for the budget-conscious to enjoy Bermuda. Cooking arrangements can vary from a fully-equipped kitchen to no facilities at all, so you must make enquiries about each property. The following selection includes some of the most charming properties.

BRIGHTSIDE

Harrington Sound
Flatts
Smiths Parish
Tel: 809-292 8410: Fax: 809-295 6968
11 units; private residence, expanded into a tourist facility; overlooks Flatts Inlet, near the Aquarium and Zoo; informal, friendly atmosphere, with private pool and barbecue facilities. $

CLEAR VIEW SUITES

Sandy Lane
Hamilton Parish
Tel: 809-293 0484; Fax: 809-293 0267
12 units; overlooks North Shore and Bailey's Bay; the perfect spot for relaxing by the pool and watching ships winding along the channel. A family business with friendly, personal attention. $

MUNRO BEACH COTTAGES

South Shore
Southampton Parish
Tel: 809-234 1175; Fax: 809-234 3528
16 units; secluded position on the waterside of Port Royal Golf Course; private beach, with coves and cliffs to explore, at Whitney Bay; tennis courts close by; appealing family atmosphere. $

Island architecture

CABANA VACATION APTS

Verdmont Road
Smith's Parish
Tel: 809-236 6964; Fax: 809-236 1829
7 units; converted 200-year-old home; private pool; barbecues frequently organised for guests; club room; accessible to beaches, Hamilton, buses and neighbourhood grocery store; very informal. $

SKY TOP

South Shore Road
Paget
Tel: 809-236 7984
11 units; a 10-minute bus ride from Hamilton, and even closer to the south beaches; hill-top property with breathtaking views. Cordial atmosphere, lovely gardens. $

ASTWOOD COVE
South Shore Road
Warwick
Tel/Fax: 809-236 0984
20 units; excellent location for beaches and on Hamilton bus route; private pool and sauna; plenty of restaurants in the area; informal and friendly. **$**

HEALTH AND EMERGENCIES

General Health
The majority of tourist-related injuries result from motorcycle accidents (*see* advice in *Getting Around* section) and sunburn. Bermuda's atmosphere is virtually pollution-free and the sun's rays penetrate without any of the usual filtering moderation. After a few hours' lying in the sun, even those with California tans get severe cases of sunburn. Regardless of screening creams, protracted periods of sunbathing is not recommended. Beware of the undertow when swimming – don't add to the work of Bermuda's efficient lifeguards.

Medical Services / Pharmacies
Bermuda is generally well served for health care. There are general practitioners and dentists throughout the island, as well as half-a-dozen pharmacies with fully qualified chemists. The telephone directory contains a complete listing.

There is only one general hospital in Bermuda: the King Edward Memorial Hospital at 7 Point Finger Road, in the central Parish of Paget (tel: 236 2345; fax: 236 2213). This is a sophisticated and fully-equipped hospital, capable of satisfying most medical needs. Cases which cannot be treated locally are evacuated by coordinated, private arrangements to the appropriate hospitals on the Eastern seaboard. Specialists make regular vis-

its from overseas. There is also a dialysis unit to treat renal patients, located opposite the main hospital entrance at 30 Point Finger Road, Paget (tel: 236 2345).

Most international medical insurance policies are recognised by the Bermuda Hospitals Board and regardless of personal coverage, no prospective patient will be rejected without preliminary treatment.

Security and Crime
There is very little crime and possessions are safer than almost anywhere in the world. In the unlikely event that you are the victim of a crime the emergency police number is, tel: 295 0011.

COMMUNICATIONS AND MEDIA

Post
The main post office is on the corner of Church Street and Parliament Street in Hamilton. Postcards and stamps can be bought and letters mailed from the picturesque Perot Post Office in Queen Street, Hamilton.

Telephones
Cable & Wireless can provide satellite link-ups to anywhere in the world. Central office: Church Street, Hamilton (tel: 297 7000; fax: 295 7909).

The island has one of the highest ratios of telephones per capita in the world; callers are connected rapidly with overseas systems for direct calls to all countries.

Area codes: US and Canada: dial 1 + regional code + telephone number. All

Beach-watch

other countries: dial 011 + country code + regional code + telephone number.

Country codes: UK: 44, France 33, Germany 49, Australia 61.

Media

There are several Bermuda radio stations and three domestic television channels. Additionally, the Bermuda Channel broadcasts directly into most hotels, carrying television programmes and information of interest to visitors. Many guest accommodations have installed 'Compuserve', a free service offering specific pictorial information on shopping, galleries, transport, etc.

Personal satellite dishes are very popular and there is an island-wide 'Cablevision' facility.

There are several local publications. The sole daily newspaper is the *Royal Gazette*. At weekends there are the *Bermuda Sun*, the *Mid Ocean News* and the *Worker's Voice*. Periodicals include the monthly magazines *RG* and *The Bermudian*. The *Bermuda Times* is a bi-weekly newspaper.

Several complimentary publications carry material targeted specifically at the visitor. Among the most widely distributed are *Bermuda Today*, *Bermuda Weekly* and *This Week in Bermuda*. *Vacation Bermuda* is a high-quality hardback book containing information of particular interest to tourists. Many major hotels have copies.

SPORT

Bermuda offers all manner of team and individual sports, ranging from powerboat racing to tennis, roadrunning and windsurfing.

September to April is dominated by football. There are several leagues and many different teams. All players are amateur. There is a National Team and international matches are played against touring sides from the Caribbean, and Central and North America. Visiting British league teams have also played against local sides.

The summer months are dominated by cricket, with regular league matches played most weekends. The season's sporting and social climax is the Cup Match, a two-day affair originally celebrating the Emancipation of the Slaves on 1 August 1834.

Spectators are welcome to watch other seasonal sporting competitions in field hockey, swimming, bowling, rugby, tennis, sailing, softball, tennis, windsurfing, power-boating, karate and many others. (*See Calendar of Special Events* section for further details.)

Golf

When golfers die they go to Bermuda – but only if they've been very good. With more golf courses per square mile than anywhere else on earth, the island merits the reputation of a golfer's paradise. There are no less then seven 18-hole courses and when you remember that the island is only 22sq miles (57sq km) in area, it is evident that you don't have to go far for a game. In fact, the only problem might be that most of the courses have such spectacular views that you might occasionally get distracted.

Bermuda's climate makes golf a pleasure all the year round, although if you are not accustomed to high temperatures you may be happier playing during the cooler winter months. Some courses offer seasonal rates, and several have reduced rates after 3pm. Naturally, some of the courses get heavily booked, so it is always advisable to call in advance. A number of tour operators offer all-in golfing holidays, some of which even include green fees and other extras.

Golfers' heaven

THE MID-OCEAN CLUB,
Tucker's Town.
Tel: 293 0330

A 6,547-yd (5,986-m) course in the Tucker's Town area; the oldest and most famous. Designed in 1921 by the former American amateur champion Charles Blair McDonald, and redesigned in 1953, it has played host to such eminent golfers as Eisenhower and Churchill. The fifth hole, Mangrove Lake, is said to be one of the best par fours in the world. The Bermuda Amateur Match Play Championship is held here each March.

THE PORT ROYAL GOLF COURSE,
Southampton
Tel: 234 0974

A 6,425-yd (5,875-m) government-owned course, where the Bermuda Open Championships are held in October each year, has spectacular views over Southampton's South Shore, and is said to be one of the best public courses in the world. There is public access to the Port Royal and to the other excellent government-owned courses on the island.

The Mid-Ocean Club and Riddell's Bay Club in Warwick are private clubs, to which you have to be introduced by a member. Other club phone numbers are:

Riddell's Bay Club, Warwick, tel: 238 1060

Belmont Hotel Club, Warwick, tel: 236 1301

Castle Harbour Golf Club, Tucker's Town, tel: 293 0795

Ocean View Golf Course, Devonshire, tel: 236 6758

Princess Golf Club, Southampton, tel: 238 0446

St George's Golf Club, St George's, tel: 297 8353

Fishing

Bermuda is a wonderful place for those who dream of fighting a marlin, or simply dangling a line over in the hopes of catching anything. Boats may be chartered through hotels, or directly through the Bermuda Charter Fishing Boat Association (tel: 292 6246). There are set prices usually based upon six paying passengers; full-day and half-day charters are available.

Underwater exploration

Water Sports

Water-skiing: Kent Richardson is Bermuda's leading international figure in this field and he has a school in Somerset (tel: 234 3354); several tour companies also organise group trips.

Snorkelling: a wonderful way to see Bermuda's underwater beauty; companies offer guided trips throughout the island. For those wishing to explore on their own, Tobacco Bay in St George is among the safest dive sites. Glass-bottom boats: prior booking is recommended for those operating out of St George or Hamilton. Many excursions operate daily.

Para-sailing: three companies offer this exhilarating experience, which is a parachute tow behind a boat: Parasail Bermuda (tel: 238 2332), Skyrider Bermuda (tel: 234 3019), and South Side Water Sports (tel: 293 2915).

Submarine dive: a fully-operational submarine embarks at Dockyard, in Somerset (tel: 234 3547).

Helmet-diving: drop beneath the waves and explore with Bronson Hartley at Flatts (tel: 292 4434).

Scuba-diving: trips for qualified swimmers visit reefs and wrecks in the company of expert divers; all the necessary equipment can be rented.

Official starter, Castle Harbour Golf Club

An island welcome

Helicopter Rides

Private trips can be arranged aboard a small helicopter operating from a helipad on the northern edge of the airport. Minimum periods of 20 minutes; must be booked in advance (tel: 295 1180).

USEFUL ADDRESSES

LOCAL VISITORS' SERVICE BUREAUX
Hamilton, tel: 295 1480
St George, tel: 297 1642
Somerset, tel: 234 1388 (summer only)
Bermuda Airport, tel: 293 076

MINISTRY OF TOURISM
Global House
43 Church Street
Hamilton, HM 12
Tel: 292 0023; fax: 292 7537
Pamphlets, maps, promotional material, lists of accredited accommodation, upcoming events and activities.

MINISTRY OF YOUTH, SPORT AND RECREATION
Old Fire Station Building
81 Court Street
Hamilton, HM 12
Tel: 292 0005; fax: 295 6292
For names and addresses of all societies, groups and organisations within its designated areas. Useful for links with sporting activities and schedules.

THE GOVERNMENT ARCHIVES
Government Administration Building
30 Parliament Street
Hamilton, HM 12
Tel: 295 5151; fax: 292 2349

Source material on Bermudian history and associated topics. This is an ideal starting point for exploring island connections. Private research is undertaken only by prior agreement.

Consulates

Most consulates consist of a local honorary appointee. Canada deploys staff regularly from its New York office. The United States maintains a permanent presence, with its own resident consul. The following countries have official consular representation: Belgium, Germany, Norway, Chile, Greece, Portugal, Denmark, Italy, Spain, Finland, Jamaica, Sweden, France, Netherlands, Switzerland.

For a list of names, addresses and telephone numbers, contact The Director, **Department of Information Services**, Global House, 43 Church Street, Hamilton HM 12, tel: 292 6384; fax: 295 5267.

FURTHER READING

Insight Guide: Bermuda, M E Zenfell, (Apa Publications, 1991).
Held in Trust, Bermuda National Trust (National Trust Publications).
The Historic Towne of St George, D F Raine, (Pompano Publications).
The Islands of Bermuda – Another World, D F Raine, (Macmillan).
Memorials of the Bermudas, Sir J H Lefroy, (Bermuda Historical Society and Bermuda National Trust – two volumes).
Bermuda Past and Present, Walter Brownell Hayward (Dodd, Mead and Company, 1910)

Index

Photography Chris Donaghue *and*
5T Jason Raine
12, 13, 14T & B Bermuda Archives

Handwriting V Barl
Cover Design Klaus Geisler
Cartography Berndtson & Berndtson

90

NOTES

INSIGHT GUIDES

COLORSET NUMBERS

You'll find the colorset number on the spine of each Insight Guide.

INSIGHT *pocket* GUIDES

• •

United States: **Houghton Mifflin Company, Boston MA 02108**
Tel: (800) 2253362 Fax: (800) 4589501

Canada: **Thomas Allen & Son, 390 Steelcase Road East**
Markham, Ontario L3R 1G2
Tel: (416) 4759126 Fax: (416) 4756747

Great Britain: **GeoCenter UK, Hampshire RG22 4BJ**
Tel: (256) 817987 Fax: (256) 817988

Worldwide: **Höfer Communications Singapore 2262**
Tel: (65) 8612755 Fax: (65) 8616438

66 I was first drawn to the Insight Guides by the excellent "Nepal" volume. I can think of no book which so effectively captures the essence of a country. Out of these pages leaped the Nepal I know – the captivating charm of a people and their culture. I've since discovered and enjoyed the entire Insight Guide Series. Each volume deals with a country or city in the same sensitive depth, which is nowhere more evident than in the superb photography. **99**

Sir Edmund Hillary

NOTES